REEL
TEARS

The Beverly Washburn Story

REEL TEARS

The Beverly Washburn Story

by Beverly Washburn and Donald Vaughn

BearManor Media
2009

Reel Tears: The Beverly Washburn Story

© 2009 Beverly Washburn and Donald Vaughan

For information, address:

BearManor Media
P. O. Box 71426
Albany, GA   31708

bearmanormedia.com

Cover design by Rick Saphire
Cover photo by Niko San-Felix

Typesetting and layout by John Teehan

Published in the USA by BearManor Media

ISBN—1-59393-348-7

Table of Contents

Dedication i

Acknowledgements.. iii

Foreword v
by Tony Dow

A Few Kind Words From Several Good Friends 1

Part One:
Hollywood, Here I Come! 9

Part Two:
So Many Show Biz Memories 21

Part Three:
Then and Now... 87

Dedication

For my wonderful, late husband Michael, I dedicate this book to you.

You were my soul-mate, my best friend, my lover, and my number one fan. Thank you for loving me unconditionally, for encouraging me to write this book, and for always showing me that the glass is "half full."

You picked me up when I was down; you made me smile when I was sad. I will forever miss your silly laugh and your wonderful bear hugs. A piece of me went with you when you died, and I will forever have a hole in my heart. Though our time together was not long enough, I treasure every moment, and I know that very few people ever know or experience the love that we had. How blessed I am that you were in my life. I will never forget you or stop loving you.

You were always so supportive and I know in my heart that you were guiding me as I wrote this book. I know you would be so proud to see it finally come to fruition.

You were my bright shining star, the love of my life, and so, my sweet Mikey, this one's for you.

From my heart,
Your honey

Acknowledgements

As I think about all of the people I would like to thank for making this book possible, it occurs to me that if I were to list each and every one, it would be a book in itself!

I would, however, like to thank my family, who have always loved me unconditionally, supported my decision to be in the wonderful, wacky world of show business, and who have always been there for me through thick and thin.

Thanks, also, to my wonderful friends, too many to list individually, but you all know who you are, and to my dear friends and colleagues Tony Dow, Paul Petersen, Sharon Baird, Cynthia Pepper, and Lauren Chapin, each of whom took the time to write something about me for this book. You have, as always, touched my heart.

To my fans, who constantly amaze me with your love and support, and the fact that, after all these years, you still want to know about my career!

To my friend and manager, Rick Saphire, who designed the cover of this book, and to my nephew, Niko, for taking the cover photo of me. You are my angel.

To my friend and manager, Laurie Jacobson, who still books me into festivals and conventions so that I can meet my fans.

To dear Kenny Miller, who put me in touch with Donald Vaughan so that this book could be written, and to Donald, a new friend, who patiently and painstakingly took my life story and put it down on paper for all to read.

To my darling friend Richard, who surprised me by buying my long lost scrapbook when it appeared on eBay, thus providing most of the photos you will find inside.

To my publisher, Ben Ohmart, who agreed without hesitation to publish this book so that my dream could come true. Thank you from my heart.

To Mike and his family, whose love sometimes makes me wonder how anyone can be as blessed as I have been.

Lastly, thanks to all of you who have bought this book so that I'm able to share a piece of my life with you. I hope you enjoy the ride as much as I have.

From my heart to yours,

– Beverly

Foreword
by Tony Dow

Beverly Washburn...Ah, what can I say about Beverly?
She's one of the sweetest people I know, possessing a rare quality. And in her autobiography, you will get an honest portrayal of her life and experiences in Hollywood as it was in the 1950s and '60s.

Nobody knows that era better than Beverly. She was there, making movies and doing live drama on television with many of the biggest stars of the day. I don't know of any child actor who worked more than Beverly. And she was one of the best; part of a small fraternity of working child actors who have a unique perspective on the Golden Age of Hollywood. Her stories are told from the heart with no judgment, favoritism, or glorification from the innocence of a child's unjaded point of view.

This is only a part of Bev's life. The world of a working child actor, with all the discipline and responsibility that comes with it, can be a burden. We have all heard stories about the problems child actors encounter during the transition to adulthood. So much is given up, so much is expected, but I've never heard Bev complain about her experiences in the entertainment industry, as she approaches her sixth decade as a dedicated actor.

Beverly and I have been friends since our early teens. She was a true product of Hollywood. She lived in Hollywood. Her family encouraged her acting. She attended a Hollywood school that allowed her to work in the film and television business.

As teenagers, we were among a small clique of Hollywood kids who ended up at the same parties, award shows, and studio gatherings. We did the phony dating scene in which press agents set up photo layouts for the popular teen magazines of the day to show us out "dating." We worked together on *Leave it to Beaver*, and she was great as one of Wally's girlfriends. And we dated for real…as I remember, quite a bit. Beverly was the only actress I was infatuated with, though I don't think she knew it at the time because I was shy around girls.

If you want to know what it was really like in Hollywood, Beverly will give you a clear picture of this oft distorted, glorified, and always glamorized world. Happy reading!

Photo courtesy of Tony Dow

A Few Kind Words From Several Good Friends

We really are a small community, this group of former kid stars...

...ranging from Silent Era performers like Baby Peggy, through the Golden Era of Hollywood, to the kids who literally grew up in front of America as television came into our homes.

But within our group, which numbers in the thousands, there is a special place reserved for those kids who day after day, year after year, turned in performances that were stunning in their intensity and power. These were the Pros, the junior "character actors" of their day, deeply respected by their peers and industry veterans alike, and atop anyone's list of child actors you could depend on was Beverly Washburn.

Some of these young artists were known for their comic abilities, or, like Beverly, their ability to reduce themselves and their audience to tears. Very few of these really gifted young performers landed roles on long-running television shows and gained "stardom," but within the Industry lists were always being kept of the true stand-outs...the kids who never failed to deliver a solid performance and who, not so incidentally, showed up on time and knew where to park!

Beverly's career is remarkable in that she competed, week after week, in grueling auditions for those plum acting jobs available to professional children during her era. In the shorthand of actresses who competed against Beverly, she had both the sizzle and the steak. You know you're good when you strike terror into the hearts of your competitors. In other words, Beverly took down more than her share of the available jobs. Her reputation as an actress was sterling even before *Old Yeller*, a signature role that I first noticed as I bawled my eyes out. Bev popped up on nearly all the shows we watched back in the day—*Wagon Train*, *77 Sunset Strip*, *Mr. Novak*, *General Electric Theater* and *Lux Video Theater*.

1

Paul and me at a publicity event. I believe it was the circus. I never went anywhere without those darned gloves!

It came to pass that circumstances brought us together in the early '60s. Beverly had grown into an attractive ingenue (love that word) and I, as a budding bubble gum star, was immersed in the publicity game, which then and now means being seen and photographed in the company of attractive women.

Even at the time, however, and the reason I approach this brief sketch of my memories of Beverly with such fondness, is that it wasn't publicity I needed, but a friend. Whether playing a highly competitive game of charades in the living room of Beverly's home with a merry band of young performers, or putting in a tedious afternoon of photo shoots, Beverly always found the time to cut through all the nonsense and, usually in a whisper, ask how I was "really doing." There were and are many secrets in the world of Young Hollywood.

To this very day my friend Beverly retains this knack. There is an "importance" to her that deserves respect. She is careful with her friends, and everlastingly faithful. It is one thing to be a good performer, but quite another to be a good person.

I can't tell you how rare this combination is in Hollywood. Beverly is always in my heart, but here's the curious thing: When I heard Beverly was featured in a recently filmed commercial, I took the time to track it down on the Internet, and you know what? She still knocks my socks off! Beverly Washburn was and still remains one of the most gifted actresses of her generation.

I write this with affection and respect.

— Paul Petersen

*   *   *

What a privilege it is to be able to write about my life with my dear friend, Beverly Washburn.

Have you ever met someone who, upon that first meeting, instantly became your friend? Someone who is beautiful, tender, sincere, gentle, funny, unassuming, gregarious, an avid pet lover, but best of all, shorter than you? That's my best friend Beverly!

We met years ago when Beverly appeared on my show, *Father Knows Best*, in an episode in which she played a poor girl that Kathy competed against in a spelling bee and, in the process, befriended. Beverly was such a professional that I was in awe of her ability.

Beverly was taller than me when we met, and had beautiful, long, blond hair, eyes that were big and blue, and wonderfully full lips. She was everything I was not, yet I was not jealous of her because she was one of those girls who put everyone at ease. Our world was very competitive so anyone who was in the same age category as you was a potential threat. Not so with Beverly. I just knew we would be friends for life.

When we first met, Beverly was a child actress with a long list of credits under her belt. I was just Billy Chapin's and Michael Chapin's kid sister who happened to land a title role on a new TV series at Columbia Studios, Screen Gems on Sunset and Gower. I was somewhat new to the business and learning the ropes, but Beverly, like my brothers, knew them well and was a seasoned professional.

Our lives were full and extremely busy so we didn't get together as often as I would have liked, but we had a lot of mutual friends. And every once in a while I'd go over to Beverly's house for one of her famous parties. It wasn't unusual to walk through Beverly's front door only to be greeted by her mom, who was precious and loving, then hoards of our childhood actor friends.

Social times were rare for me because of my work schedule, so Beverly's parties were something I looked forward to. On any given night you might find Bobby Diamond (*Fury*), Sandy Descher (who played Bev's sister on *The New Loretta Young Show*), Steve Benson (a child actor whose mom also happened to be the casting director at Desilu Productions), Johnny Washbrook (*My Friend Flicka*), Paul Petersen (*The Donna Reed Show*), the kids from *The Mickey Mouse Club*, Johnny Crawford (*The Rifleman*), Barbara Parkins, Cindy Carol, Dirk and Dack Rambo, Randy Boone, Eddie Hodges, Steve Stevens, Tommy Kirk…the list goes on and on.

In 1964, Beverly and I found ourselves competing against each other in the Deb Star Ball, a very prestigious Hollywood coming-out party in which participants were sponsored by a studio and presented to Hollywood society. Participants were interviewed, just like in the Miss America Pageant, and there were different categories on which we were graded. I won the "Most Beautiful Legs" division, while Beverly got to wear the white Ball Gown and meet all of the dignitaries.

That was the first and last time Beverly and I competed for the same thing because I left the business shortly after. Beverly, however, continued to study her craft. In fact, I don't think she has ever stopped working! I always tell people that while Beverly is not an actress who has been on a long-running series, she has done more shows than many of us, and she is a professional at her craft. That's why I look up to her so much.

Beverly and I didn't see each other for many years, but finally reconnected in 1988. I was in Hawaii ministering (I had become a licensed and ordained evangelist in the interim) and Beverly and Mike, her darling husband, were visiting Beverly's sister, Audrey, on Kauai. We ran into each other at the Fern Grotto, and it was like old times.

Mike was the cat's meow and so adoring of Bev. He was good-looking, funny, and fit Beverly perfectly. They were so much in love that it seemed to just ooze out of them. It was only by chance that we met, but I knew Bev and I would have a lifelong friendship.

It was in Hawaii that Beverly first met my daughter, Summer. Summer was 7 years old at the time and she just fell in love with Beverly and Mike, so much so that she asked Beverly if she could call her "aunt!" I was flabbergasted and looked at Beverly with an expression that said, "I think she really likes you!" Beverly was touched and graciously said yes. To this day, some 23 years later, Beverly is still known as "Aunt Beverly," not just to Summer, but to my son, Matthew, as well.

After several days together on Kauai, I had to leave for Diamond Head on the island of Oahu, where Summer and I had another evangelical meeting. Beverly and I exchanged phone numbers and promised we'd stay in touch, especially since she and Mike were moving to Dallas and my family and I lived in Killeen, which was only three hours away. We kissed, we hugged, we said our goodbyes, and Summer and I left. We would miss our dear "Aunt Beverly."

Almost a year later, Beverly called. She and Mike had settled into their beautiful house just outside of Dallas, so Matthew, Summer, and I drove up and spent the day with them. Upon entering Mike and Beverly's house, we were greeted by at least a dozen little four-legged creatures, dogs and cats alike.

My kids and I laughed because at home on our "ranch" I took in animals from the ASPCA and found them homes, though I kept most of them for myself. So a love of animals was just another thing Beverly and I had in common that would bring us even closer. Of course, we had a wonderful time catching up. Sadly, not too long after, Mike and Beverly moved to Las Vegas.

A few years later, both Bev's sister, Audrey, and her wonderful husband, Mike, died from cancer. Not long after, my sister-in-law of 40 years developed cancer and passed away as well. Beverly and I were drawn together as dear friends dealing with the pain of losing people we deeply loved. My family's prayers, support, and love were there for Beverly, and even in her pain, she was there for me.

Many a tear has been shed between us. We comfort each other, and Beverly is one of the best comforters I know. These very sad times in our lives have made us even stronger friends; the love flows freely, unabashedly toward and for each other. We've come through as child actors, married women, and dearest of friends, and now we are headed to the other side. Stronger, wiser, funnier (if that is even possible) and happier!

Beverly is the sister I never had, a second aunt to my children, and the Rock of Gibraltar for all of us. And best of all, she's still shorter than me! Even if it is only by an inch.

– Lauren Chapin

*   *   *

I consider it an honor to be asked to write about Beverly Washburn. She and I first met at her 18th birthday party. Neither of us can remember how that came about, but we're sure glad that it did.

We lost contact for about 30 years, but ran into each other at an autograph show in Los Angeles and were delighted to see each other again. We had many, many years to catch up on and from then on we made sure we stayed in contact with each other.

Beverly and I have become the best of friends. In fact, I call her my "Little Sis." We've shared many years of good times and sad, but through it all, Beverly always puts her friends' problems and feelings before her own.

One thing that means a lot to both of us is our love for animals. We know we can count on each other to understand and sympathize when one of our four-legged "kids" is sick or having a bad day.

Cynthia, Paul Petersen and me at a Friends of Old Time Radio
convention in Newark, New Jersey. Photo courtesy of Rick Saphire.

Beverly is a wonderful actress, as anyone who has seen her work will
attest, but most importantly to me, Beverly is a wonderful lady and a true
friend.

– Cynthia Pepper

*   *   *

Without a doubt, Beverly Washburn is one of the greatest actresses I
have ever known. She has captured every part she has played since childhood, when she was known as the girl who could cry on cue, to current
times.

Beverly and I first met at the Walt Disney Studio, where she was
filming *Old Yeller* and I was filming *The Mickey Mouse Club*. We became

fast friends from the moment we met while attending school in the studio's little red trailers, and now, more than 50 years later, we are still close friends.

Throughout the years we have shared so much of life together, as well as many, many tears—some from sorrow and some from laughter. I can't imagine getting through life without Beverly's friendship. She has been a loving, caring, devoted, giving, and loyal friend—my chosen sister in life. Beverly has collected angels for years and I believe it is because she is such an angel herself.

Our lives seem to have run on a similar path. Neither of us had children and, therefore, we are great lovers of animals. As children, Bev worked with Jack Benny; I worked with Eddie Cantor. We both worked as actresses in Hollywood at a young age. Neither of our parents pressured us into our careers; it was something we both loved and had fun doing.

During our teenage years, we attended various teen magazine date parties, played in a young Hollywood bowling league along with Paul Petersen (we called ourselves the Gutter Getters), had sleep-overs at each other's houses, and ate plenty of ice cream!

Later, Beverly married the love of her life, Michael Radell, who also became my dear friend. The three of us shared many wonderful memo-

Me and Sharon at the Hotel del Coronado in San Diego, Christmas 2008.

ries together, all of which are stored within my heart. Dealing with Mike's death was one of our greatest challenges. His passing has left a big hole in Beverly's heart.

Now, so many years later, Beverly and I are still extremely close. We enjoy traveling together, sipping wine, and sharing tears of both sorrow and joy. And, of course, eating ice cream! Thank you, my darling friend Beverly. I've loved all of our years together.

– Sharon Baird

Part One
Hollywood, Here I Come!

Every good story should start at the beginning, and this one is no different.

I was born on Thanksgiving Day, November 25, 1943, at Hollywood Presbyterian Hospital in Los Angeles, California. I was the youngest of five children, and came as a surprise to my parents (my mother thought she had the flu) because they were already grandparents to my sister Dorothy's daughter, Darlene, and to my brother Howard's son, Howard III.

My mother was born in Milwaukee and my dad was from Chicago. They met when they were 17; my mother's family moved next door to my dad's family. They lived in Chicago after they got married, but moved west when my sister, Audrey, became ill. The doctor thought she might have polio (she didn't) and suggested that they move to a warmer climate for her health. My mother's sister, Emma, who was the cutest person who ever lived, was living in Los Angeles, so it was decided that the family would relocate there.

I didn't come from a traditional show biz family, although my dad's brothers and sisters were in vaudeville. My mother never worked, staying home instead to raise me and my four siblings. My dad held various jobs, none of which really amounted to much of anything, so for a very long time we had little by way of material possessions. One thing we did have, however, was plenty of love and laughter. My dad had a great sense of humor and it seemed like he was forever telling jokes (clean ones, at least in front of the kids) and I remember that he would drag them out forever. Another fond memory of my childhood is how everyone hugged and how my parents were always holding hands.

The house that I grew up in on Fuller Avenue was in a nice middle-class neighborhood, though certainly not what you would consider a wealthy neighborhood. My sisters, brothers, and I were blessed with a lot of friends, and they always wanted to come to our house to play because my mother always insisted on feeding everybody. She loved to make pancakes and the coffee pot was always on. (I started drinking coffee at 16 and have been addicted to it ever since.) My mother never seemed to mind sharing whatever food we had. One of her favorite sayings was, "We may have to split a bean, but you're welcome to it," and she meant it.

Speaking of food, I shudder when I think of what we ate! I don't recall ever eating salads, fresh fruits, or vegetables. Instead, our diet consisted primarily of sugary doughnuts, pancakes, white bread, macaroni and cheese, and the like. We were brought up to eat everything on our plate because of the starving children in other countries (though for the life of me, I could never figure out how my eating everything on *my* plate would help those poor, starving kids). Perhaps that's why I always seemed to have a bit of a weight problem. Fortunately, it never developed into an actual eating disorder; I just had to be careful of what I ate. I never met a dessert that I didn't like, and I like to tease that "I have an hour glass figure—with 45 minutes at the bottom!"

Christmas at our house holds some of the fondest memories of my childhood. My family never had much money, but when it came to Christmas, it was all about "giving." We would typically celebrate on Christmas Eve, either at our house on Fuller Avenue, my sister Dorothy's house or my brother Howie's house. We would always have chili for dinner (we couldn't afford the traditional turkey) and the tree would be covered with presents—so many that they would practically fill the room. We also had gifts for our many friends who dropped by.

Now, if you were to calculate the cost of all of the presents under the tree, it would probably total around $11, as they were mostly socks for the guys and maybe lotion from the local dime store for the girls, but boy, did we have fun opening them! I remember one Christmas Eve when my nephew

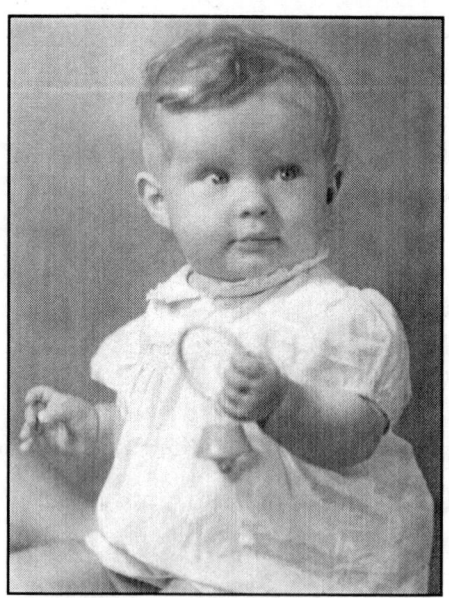

Me at 6 months old.

Howard received so many socks that he began draping them up and down his arms and legs, around his neck and even on his head. Every time he opened a gift, it seemed as if it had more socks in it! The image of Howard covered in socks makes me smile to this day.

There was always music, love and laughter, making it one of the best times of the year for my family and our friends. I have very fond memories of my daddy at Christmastime. He would always tell the same corny jokes, which inevitably filled the house with gales of laughter.

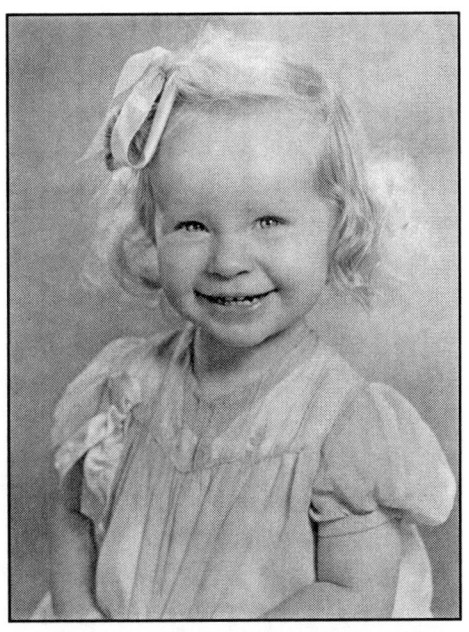

Me at age 2. I was such a happy child!

Christmas morning was when Santa delivered his presents. None of the gifts was wrapped, they were just sitting under the tree as if St. Nick had taken them from his sleigh and placed them there. I smile at the amount of effort that my parents put into ensuring that we all believed in Santa Claus, which made our Christmases brighter. As a young child, I delighted in the fact that the cookies and milk I left out were always gone in the morning.

Like many youngsters, I believed in Santa Claus for quite a long time – until Tommy Rettig, with whom I worked on a show called *Heart of Gold*, finally told me that Santa didn't exist. I was devastated, and I don't think I ever forgave him!

Even now, there are times when my friends and I will reflect on those magical Christmases. Over the years, many friends have told me that they are some of the fondest memories they have of my family and home.

The first house in which we lived had only two bedrooms, so my sister, Audrey, and I had to share even though she was eight years older. My brother, George, had to camp out on the sofa and times were lean. Across the street was a big beautiful white house with a pointed roof and beautiful rose trees up the walkway. My mother was always part daydreamer and part positive thinker. She used to say, "One day we're all going to live in that big white house!" Of course, none of us believed her, primarily because a family was already living there, the house wasn't for sale, and even if it was, we didn't have the money to buy it.

That is, until my acting career really took off. Once I became a fairly established name in Hollywood, our financial situation eased. Well, you guessed it. The beautiful white house on the corner of Fuller and Hawthorne, one block from Hollywood Boulevard and one block from Sunset Boulevard, came on the market. My parents bought it and in we moved, just as my mother had predicted! I lived there until I was 23 and I finally moved out and got my own apartment.

My parents had a wonderful marriage and had been together for 43 years when my dad died. Considering the strength of my parents' marriage, it seems odd that both of my sisters were married three times, one brother was married three times, and my other brother and I were both married twice. I have no recollection of my parents ever fighting in front of us (if they ever fought at all, which I doubt) or even raising their voices to us or each other. My parents instilled in us good, old-fashioned family values, including the importance of two simple phrases—please and thank you.

Me at age 13 with my wonderful father and mother.

Such kindness extended to my mother's relationship with the various cast and crew with whom I worked as a child. "Hollywood stage mother" often has a bad connotation, which I understand because prima donna stage mothers can make everyone's life hell. However, my mother was anything but. She was well-liked by all of the crew wherever I worked because she never interfered and sat quietly in the background while I did my job. However, at the risk of sounding disrespectful, my mother was a little "ditzy," much like Gracie Allen was.

She and my eldest sister, Dorothy, were extremely close. My mother gave birth to Dor-

othy at the tender age of 18, and
they were more like sisters than
mother and daughter. When Dorothy died from lung cancer at the
age of 58, my mother never really recovered and started going
downhill until she died in a convalescent home at age 83.

Dorothy and I were never
particularly close, though we loved
each other, and for reasons I still
don't understand, she was absolutely
horrible to me when she drank.
When she was sober, she was funny
and lovable, but she was a very mean
drunk and I would dread her
phone calls, which typically ended
with her yelling at me for no reason and telling me that I was "nothing." Her husband, George, would
take the phone away from her and

Me and my sister Audrey, who was my best
friend and angel. I was modeling for Debby
Ross fashions when this photo was taken.

apologize to me, saying that she was drunk and didn't mean it. This went on for
most of my teenage years and into adulthood. I cried every time I got those
calls and to this day I don't understand what brought out that reaction in her. I
know in my heart that she loved me, but alcohol can do terrible things to
people. My brother, George, was also an alcoholic, but he was never mean. In
fact, the more he drank, the funnier and sweeter he became. (My oldest brother,
Howie, and I loved each other, too, but because of the 24-year age gap, he was
more like an uncle than a brother.)

Audrey was the sister I most looked up to. She had the sweetest
smile and a temperament to match. She was my rock every time there
was a crisis in my life, such as when I divorced my first husband. No
matter what the problem, Audrey was there for me. She was extremely
supportive and proud of everything I did. I've been told that it's not
normal when siblings never argue, but I swear that with Audrey and me,
it's true. And the same for Georgie and me.

Because I've always been rather petite (I'm only 5'1") Audrey nicknamed
me "Teency-Weencie," which she later shortened to just "Weencie." My nick-

name for her was "Chummy." I have no idea how that name came about, but I started calling her that from the time I could first speak and it just stuck.

After moving to California, Audrey's health improved and she eventually became an entertainer. In the 1950s she went on tour with Gene Autry as a backup singer, and she later sang backup with Marlene Dietrich in Las Vegas. She also went on tour with a group called Bill Norvis and the Upstarts, which included Bill, Audrey, Audrey's friend Laurie, Gary Clarke, and Tony Butala. (Gary went on to star in *The Virginian*, while Tony later became a member of The Lettermen.) Audrey was also Penny Marshall's stand-in on *Laverne & Shirley*, and had roles in *The Lion in Winter*, starring Peter O'Toole and Katharine Hepburn, and *The Law and Mr. Jones*, starring James Whitmore.

In a roundabout way, Audrey's showbiz career led me into show business as well. When I was about 5 years old, my mother and I accompanied Audrey to a dance gig at the Capitol Theatre in Yakima, Washington. At the request of the MC in the club where Audrey and her troupe were performing, I was brought out on stage and sang "I'm A Big Girl Now." It was great fun, and I wasn't nervous at all. In fact, I had a blast.

I felt comfortable in front of an audience, and my mother immediately realized my potential. Eager to get me into showbiz like Audrey, she took it upon herself to get me an agent. And not just any agent, but the renowned Lola Moore, who represented many of the best-known child performers in Hollywood. My mother tried to contact Lola by phone, and was immediately given the brush off. Lola had a huge stable of performers and wasn't looking to add any more. However, my mother refused to take no for an answer, so one day she dressed me up and we took the bus to Hollywood and Lola's office, which wasn't far from the Paramount lot.

To call my mother tenacious would be an understatement. We walked into Lola's office and were met by a receptionist who gave us a wary eye. My mother lied and said that we had an appointment with Lola that morning. The receptionist looked at the schedule and saw no mention of our name. "You must be mistaken," she said.

"I don't think so," my mother said. "If you'll get her on the phone, I'm sure we can straighten everything out."

"I'm sorry, I can't," the receptionist said. "She's at 20th Century Fox and won't be back for hours."

My mother smiled. "We'll wait," she said.

By 11:30, the waiting room was filled with about a dozen equally determined mothers, most of whom we assumed also did not have an appointment. This meant that when Lola arrived, it would be bedlam. "This won't do," Mom muttered. She took me by the hand and walked by the receptionist's desk. On the wall was a photo of a rotund woman standing in front of an elegant automobile. "Tell me, is that Miss Moore?" Mom asked.

The girl turned and smiled. "Yes, it is." she said.

"And is that her car?"

"Yes it is. An original pre-war Packard Convertible."

"What color is it?" Mom asked, since the photo was in black and white.

With seeming pride, the receptionist answered, "Fire engine red. You can't miss it."

That was all my mother needed. Now she knew what Lola looked like, what time she was expected, the make and color of her car, and she intuitively felt that Lola would probably park in back. She and I made a beeline for the rear of the building and waited in the shade of a tree. Sure

enough, about a half hour later the gleaming red convertible pulled into a private space and the most formidable-looking woman either of us had ever seen stepped out. She must have weighed 300 pounds, and she was wearing a huge hat, just like in the photograph in her office.

After gathering a briefcase and a few bound screenplays from the back of her car, Lola moved toward the back door of her office. Mom cut her off at the pass.

"Miss Moore?" she asked.

A preoccupied Lola looked up. "Yes?"

"Miss Moore, I only want you to take one look at my daughter. Just two seconds of your time."

"Do you have an appointment?" Lola asked. "I only work by appointment."

Up to now, Lola had pointedly avoided looking at me. "I wasn't able

Me modeling for Little M'Lady Fashions. I was 3 ½ years old.

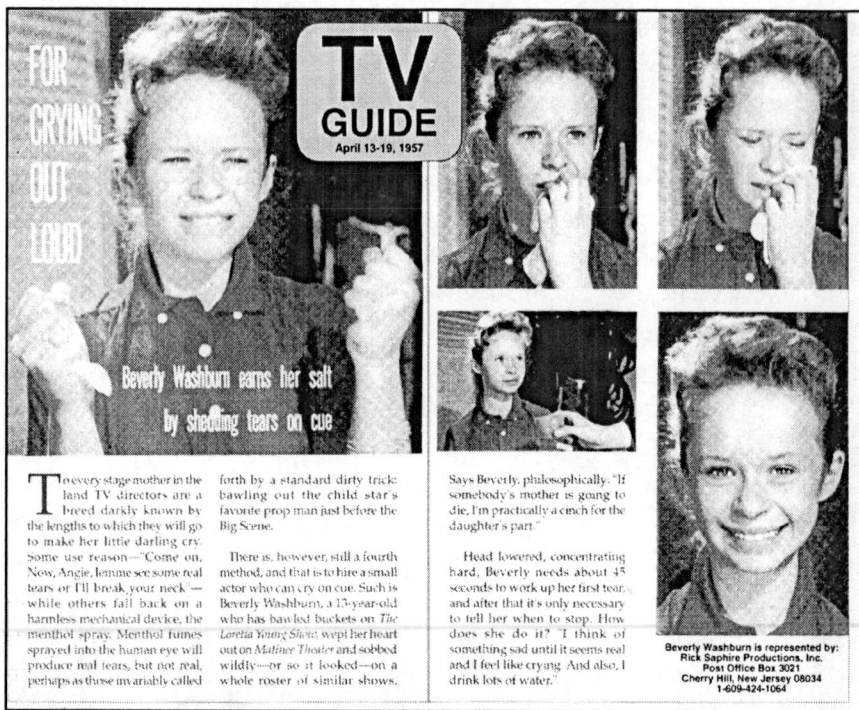

A two-page profile of me from *TV Guide*, which focused on my ability to cry on cue. It's a skill that has served me well as an actress.

to get one," Mom said. "Your secretary told me you were too busy."

"Well, that's the truth. I'm afraid I can't do anything for you now. Call me back. I may be able to work you in next month."

My mother drew in her breath, preparing to tell Lola about my appearance in Yakima and some earlier work I had done modeling children's clothes for Little M'Lady Fashions. But just then I stepped forward. "I sure like your hat, Miss Moore," I said, beaming with the biggest smile I could muster. Lola looked down at me, and suddenly she became a whole new person.

"Well," Lola replied, "you're about the only one who does. Know why I wear such large hats?"

I shook my head. "No, ma'am, I don't."

"It's my signature. I want people to know I'm around. I want them to see me coming." As she said this, she kept looking directly into my eyes.

"I don't know how they could miss you anyway," I said innocently.

Lola roared, her body shaking with each gale of laughter. "Well, why are we standing here?" she said, tears streaming down her face. "Come on in to the office. I think I can lay my hands on some lemonade."

After pushing back a scheduled appointment and ordering some refreshments, Lola came right to the point. "There's a lot of work to be done," she said. "Even with Beverly's winning features, we don't know if she's photogenic, and I certainly don't know if she has any acting ability."

Mom told her about my performance at the Capitol Theater, and my modeling gigs for Little M'Lady Fashions.

"Well, that's all to the good, but it isn't enough," Lola said. "What I'd like to do before we go any further is sign an interim contract and get her started with a drama coach."

Mom was aghast. She hadn't expected this to happen so quickly. "Do you have anyone special in mind?" she asked.

"Of course. Her name is Mildred Gardner, and if she can't bring the actress out in Beverly, nobody can."

Mom agreed and Lola made the call to Mildred. I was on my way to becoming a star.

Mildred and Mom hit if off right away, and I fell in love with Mildred too. For the next six months, as frequently as we could, I took voice training (diction, breathing, euphony, enunciation) as well as instruction in gestures, expression, body movement, and control, which I had mastered even before taking Mildred's classes. I thought the instruction was a lot of fun, and it all seemed to come so naturally to me. It was in her classes that I perfected my ability to cry on cue, a skill that would serve me well throughout my career. Later, when asked how I did it, I always explained, "I think of whatever it is I'm supposed to be crying about and invariably it makes me cry." Years later, TV Guide wrote a two-page article about me titled "Beverly Washburn Earns Her Salt by Crying on Cue."

After Mildred had taught me everything she could, she said I was ready, and that she felt if I continued studying, it would take away my naturalness. Now it was up to Lola to get me work.

Maybe it's the ham in me … but I always loved being in front of the camera. My parents were always supportive of my desire to be a professional actress; they encouraged me but never pushed me. I can think of nothing sadder than a child actor who is in the business because his or her parents are forcing them or living vicariously through them.

I recall doing a television show with another child actor who really did not want to be there. He wanted to be out playing with his friends and I remember so vividly his mother shaking him and telling him to get in front of the camera. That experience deeply affected me because al-

A publicity shot at age 12.

though I was young myself—around 10—I was so happy to be there and he was crying as his mother was shaking him. I truly felt sorry for him.

My parents always told me that just because I was an actress, that didn't make me any better than anyone else. A little luckier, perhaps, but not better, and they always said that as long as I was happy working, kept up my grades, and performing didn't go to my head, then I could work as long as I wanted. They meant it, too. Even though I was my family's primary source of income, I still had to do my chores.

Many people have asked me how I kept my head on straight when so many of my peers fell by the wayside, opting for drugs, alcohol, and the like. I really feel that it was due to my upbringing. Though my parents weren't particularly well educated, nor did we have much money, we had values, and for that I'm grateful.

As I started working more and more as an actress, I just assumed the role of family bread winner. My parents bought a house with the money I made and, of course, every year they bought a new car. Looking back, I know they truly loved me and weren't exploiting me, but common sense would suggest that the smart thing would have been for them to put away some of that money for me when I got older. I think that they thought the money would *always* be coming in and that maybe, one day, I would become a really big star and that there would be no problem. I'm not sure if I'm being naive or trying to protect them, but in my heart I really don't think they knew what they were doing, yet it came back to haunt my family years later.

Even though I made very good money as an actress, I had little to call my own by the time I was old enough to claim it because my parents, through poor business decisions, had spent almost all of it. People sometimes ask me if I was horrified by that knowledge, or if I was angry at my parents for losing what was rightfully mine. I tell them no, because I know in my heart that what they did wasn't done out of malice or greed, but because they simply didn't understand the long-term consequences of the decisions they made while I was a child. My parents got married in their teens after dropping out of school and they just didn't know how to handle money.

By the time I co-starred in *The New Loretta Young Show* (don't feel bad if you don't remember it—it aired opposite *Ben Casey*, so it didn't last very long), the so-called Jackie Coogan Law had gone into effect so my parents were required to place a certain percentage of my income in a trust fund until I turned 21. The law was a lifesaver for a lot of young actors because it was designed to protect child performers from greedy parents, managers, or agents.

Our situation was very different. My father became very ill when I was 19. He had diabetes and also had a kidney removed, and he wasn't expected to live. Since my mother never worked and my father couldn't, it was up to me to free up the money for his care. I went to court and asked permission to tap the money in my trust fund so that I could pay my dad's hospital bills. There was a hearing and my request was granted. I took out all the money I had saved and gave it to the hospital. Then *The New Loretta Young Show*, my primary source of income, was cancelled. Do I regret taking the money out of my trust fund? Not in the least, because my father was my hero. He died a year later, when I was 20, but at least I was able to give him one more year.

The truth is, I never really thought much about money, and I never worried about my future. My mother's philosophy was that God would always provide. I assumed that philosophy, too, but learned the hard way that sometimes you have to meet God half way.

Part Two
So Many Show Biz Memories

When I first entered the profession, being a child actress was a lot different than it is today.

For one thing, the amount of money that child performers make today is astronomical compared to what I typically received. For many of my jobs I earned $250 a week. That's not a lot today, but back then it was pretty good. Of course, it's all relative. When I was a child you could buy a gallon of gas for 37 cents and a quart of milk for 22 cents. I believe that everyone should make good money, but the money paid to a lot of today's actors is a bit excessive, in my opinion. Is it really necessary for a performer to make $1 million a week when there is so much poverty in the world? I know that there are many celebrities who give back, but I often wonder just how many of them regularly give to charities. One of the reasons I love to appear at autograph shows is that it gives me a chance to raise money for my favorite animal charities.

My first big acting job was a movie titled *The Killer That Stalked New York* (1950), starring Evelyn Keyes. I remember driving onto the Columbia lot my first day and going onto the sound stage. Everything seemed so huge, and I was mesmerized by the sets. They had no ceiling and there were lights, cables, and equipment everywhere. When I did my first scene, it all seemed so natural to me, perhaps because my best friend, Joanie, and I had done our very own version of improv when we played together.

Joanie lived down the street from me, so we would play often. Usually we would start with standard kids' games like hide and go seek and hopscotch, but invariably we would play our favorite game, which we made up, called "Bob and Dick." Bob and Dick were our imaginary husbands. Joanie pretended she was Jane Powell and I pretended to be Debbie Reynolds. We entertained ourselves for hours playing that game. Not only did it help my acting skills, but it also stimulated my imagination.

Joanie and I are still best friends to this day. Our lives back then seemed to mirror each other: we looked alike, dressed alike, and sometimes we would pretend we were twins. Her older sister, Jackie, and my older sister, Audrey, were friends and they toured together with Gene Autry when they were 18. My older brother, George, was friends with Joanie's brother, Chuck, and my parents were friends with Joanie's parents, Olive and Lester. Joanie and I did everything the same and vowed to be friends forever. But as we got older, our lives went in totally different directions. Joanie got married at the age of 19 (I was her maid of honor) and had three beautiful children, became a concert violinist, and had been married to her husband for almost 40 years when he died. I, on the other hand, didn't get married until my late 20s, got divorced, then lived with someone for seven years, then got married again. It's amazing how our lives could be so different and yet today we are as close as ever. It saddens us deeply to know that someday one of us will lose the other.

Anyway, *The Killer That Stalked New York* was a long, long time ago, but I still have vivid memories of my audition for it. I remember arriving at the waiting room and being given the "sides," which is sort of a mini script of the scene you're about to read for. It read: "Sitting in the lobby is little Walda Kowalski with her long brown hair and her big brown eyes." The color of my eyes and hair was not particularly relevant to the scene, but that's the way the writer had written it, and sometimes such directions play an important role in casting. As a result, my mother turned to me and said, "Honey, you're not what they're looking for because they want someone with brown hair and brown eyes and you have blonde hair and blue eyes. But just go in there and do your best and don't be sad if you don't get the part. One of these days you will." Even though I was just 6 years old, I could already read well and I had a photographic memory, so I read the sides and learned my lines and I was ready to go.

A few minutes later, none other than Jock Mahoney walked through the lobby where my mother and I were waiting. He stopped to say hello because Audrey and I had met him a few months earlier at a special benefit for war veterans. He asked my mother what I was doing there and she told him that I was auditioning for the part of the little girl in *The Killer That Stalked New York*. Jock was under contract to Columbia at the time and had some clout, so he went to the producer and told him that I had done this and I had done that—none of which was true! So

Me and Evelyn Keyes in a scene from my very first movie, *The Killer That Stalked New York*. The shooting title was *Frightened City*.

basically, Jock Mahoney lied for me, they took his word for it, and I got the part. I was very grateful because it's always hard to get that first break. I had been on countless auditions but never got the part because I had no acting experience and no one wanted to take a chance on me. But once I had that first part under my belt (with dialogue), it was easier to land other roles, so I really owe everything to Jock.

We got the call later that afternoon from my agent, Lola Moore, that I had landed the role, and I was told to report to wardrobe the next day. My parents were beside themselves and I was also very happy to have been cast. The next day we drove up to the guard gate and were told that we could drive right onto the lot. I was fitted for my wardrobe and we went home. My parents were on cloud nine. The idea that we were actually allowed to drive onto the Columbia Studio lot seemed surreal to them.

Even though I was only 6 and had a very small part, I was treated like a princess and very thrilled to be there. I went into makeup, which was fun for me as I had never had makeup on other than to play "dress up" with Joanie. It wasn't lipstick or eye makeup, just foundation, which they always apply so you will photograph well. But for me, sitting in the makeup chair was just like playing dress up! Then they sent me to the hair department, where a stylist put my hair into little curls. (Not quite as cute as Shirley Temple, but we tried.) From there I was introduced to what they called the "welfare worker," a certified school teacher from the Los Angeles Board of Education. Her job, in addition to actually teaching classes to young performers, was to make sure that a child's welfare was well protected. Before I was allowed to work, I had to go to the Los Angeles Board of Education for a physical and to receive a work permit. This was something that had to be done every six months to make sure that I was physically able to work and that I had no health problems.

Child actors are allowed to work only so many hours a day, and never overtime. You have to have three hours of schooling a day, which you bring from your own school, and you have to have schooling in at least 20 minute increments. This means a director can pull a child out of school to do a scene as long as he or she has done at least 20 minutes of class work, but not if the child has done less than 20 minutes at a time. Once you've completed three hours, you're done for the day.

I met my teacher, did my 20 minutes of school work, and then I was escorted to the set. My scene was with Evelyn Keyes. Of course, because I was so young, that meant nothing to me, and it wasn't until I got older that I realized just how famous my co-star really was! Evelyn was very nice to me. In our scene together I admire a pretty broach she's wearing and she gives it to me. Unfortunately, I contract small pox from our encounter because Evelyn's character is a carrier, hence the title of the movie: *The Killer That Stalked New York*. In my next scene, I'm shown in an oxygen tent, then I die. For proper effect, the makeup people made me look a little more pale, though, because the movie was in black and white, the makeup was actually grayish. The whole experience was so much fun for me, and I got to enjoy a very dramatic death.

My first experience in motion pictures went quite well, and I was on the way to a very promising career. But over the years I learned that not everyone in Hollywood was nice, even if they smile at you. In fact, Hollywood can sometimes bring out the very worst in people.

For example, when I was just starting out and had done only a few things, I was on an audition for a part and Nick Adams (whose real name was Nick Adamshock) also happened to be in the waiting room trying to get his big break. My mother, being the friendly type, struck up a conversation with him and told him that my brother was about the same age as he.

Nick then confessed that he had come to Los Angeles to break into show business and was sleeping in his car because he had no money. Well, that's all it took. The next thing I knew, Nick Adams was at our house, sleeping on the floor in our living room and eating every meal with us. My mother told him that he would never go hungry as long as she was around, and he could always "split a bean" with us, which he did many times.

Nick and my brother, George, became good friends and hung out together. George was a starving actor as well, trying out for various roles and even working at times as a stunt man, extra, and stand-in, which is someone hired to "stand in" for the actors while the lighting and other technical issues are set up. Typically, a stand-in is hired because he looks like the actor he is standing in for. He will be about the same size and have the same hair color so the lighting will be just right when filming begins. I mention this because George looked somewhat like Nick in size and hair color and when Nick was "discovered" and landed his own show, George called him to see if he could get him a part, even as an extra or as Nick's stand-in. Sadly, fame had immediately gone to Nick's head because suddenly he wouldn't give George the time of day. It's sad, considering how my family had taken Nick in when he had nothing at all, fed him and given him a place to sleep. I've never been able to figure out how someone can turn his back like that on people who were so kind to him. George was one of the nicest guys you'd ever meet, and Nick's refusal to even take his phone calls tore him apart.

Years later, George stood in for Donald O'Connor and also became good friends with Robert Fuller. He also starred with me in the Jack Hill film *Pit Stop* (1969), playing Ellen Burstyn's husband. (At the time, Ellen went by the name of Ellen McRae.) I'm proud to say that George was wonderful in that movie. When he died in 1991, my heart was broken. He was one of my heroes, and probably one of the funniest people I've ever known; no one could tell a joke like he could. Losing Georgie (as I called him) was beyond devastating. Though he was eleven years older than me, we were extremely close and never had a cross word. Not many siblings can say that, I believe.

A few years ago, shortly before he passed away, I ran into Donald O'Connor at a Jack and Jills luncheon held at the Sportsman's Lodge in Los Angeles. I went to introduce myself and the first thing Donald said was, "How is George? I've lost touch with him." I told him the sad news that George had passed away, and Donald gave me a big hug and said he was honored to have known him. Donald's kindness touched me deeply.

A lobby card from *Superman and the Mole Men*, one of my earliest movies.
That's me sitting on the floor holding a ball.

After I finished *The Killer That Stalked New York*, I continued to go
on auditions, which were a little easier now that I had a "big" credit to my
name. My next film was *Superman and the Mole Men* (1951) with George
Reeves and Phyllis Coates. My role certainly wasn't as impressive as *The
Killer That Stalked New York*, but I didn't care—I was having a blast.

For those who have seen *Superman and the Mole Men*, I'm the little
girl who's in bed when the Mole Men (actually, the diminutive radioactive
denizens of a mysterious underground world who come to the surface via a
very deep oil well) come into my bedroom through a window. I talk with
them, then we innocently play with a ball together. My mother walks in,
sees me with the Mole Men, and screams hysterically. End of scene.

My memories of *Superman and the Mole Men* are a little hazy, considering how much time has passed, but I do remember thinking how
cute the actors who played the Mole Men were. However, apparently not
everyone felt that way. Not too long ago, I was doing an autograph signing and a guy about my age walked up to my table. He looked at the
photo I had from *Superman and the Mole Men* and said, "I saw that when
I was a kid and those Mole Men scared the crap out of me!" But I didn't
find them scary at all, just cute. Jerry Maren, who also appeared as a

Munchkin in *The Wizard of Oz*, played one of the Mole Men. The others were played by John T. Bambury, Tony Boris, and Billy Curtis.

Superman and the Mole Men was filmed as a (rather short) feature film, but ended up as a two-part episode in the first season of *Adventures of Superman*, which ran for six successful seasons and was syndicated for many years after. The series had a painfully small budget, but ended up having a tremendous cultural impact, and I'm so grateful to have been a part of it.

I've been asked over the years what it was like to work with George Reeves. I was really young, so working with George had no meaning to me, though seeing him on the set in his Superman costume meant the world, and was a thrill that I'll never forget. To me, George really was Superman! It wasn't until years later that I truly understood what a special moment that had been. Talk about cool! I feel the same way about having been directed by Cecil B DeMille, George Stevens, Stanley Kramer, and Frank Capra. All are revered Hollywood legends, and deservedly so. But when you're only 7 or 8, it just doesn't have the same impact. Now, as an adult, I realize how blessed I was to even meet them, let alone be directed by them.

In 1952, I appeared in an episode of *Ford Television Theater* titled "Heart of Gold," starring Edmund Gwenn, Anita Louise, Tommy Rettig (who later played Timmy on *Lassie*), and none other than George Reeves

George Reeves gives me a magical locket in an episode of *Ford Television Theater* titled "Heart of Gold."

as my father! It was a thrill to see him again, and he was just the nicest man. He remembered me from *Superman and the Mole Men* and was so receptive. In the show, Edmund Gwenn played a snowman who comes to life when my brother (Tommy) and I are building him, and I give him my heart-shaped locket. The effects crew had created a very realistic snowman suit out of cotton for Edmund, and he looked great in it.

An autographed picture from Bing Crosby, with whom I co-starred in *Here Comes the Groom*.

I always felt fortunate to have worked with George Reeves not once, but twice, and was shocked and saddened by his death in 1959, ostensibly a suicide. In recent years, I've done autograph shows with Phyllis Coates, who was the series' first Lois Lane, as well as with Noel Neill, who took over when Phyllis left the series, and both have said that they can't possibly imagine that George would have taken his own life. Some have suggested that George was murdered, but I guess the mystery will never truly be solved.

After *Superman and the Mole Men* I was called to do a screen test for the part of Suzie, the French war orphan who is adopted by Bing Crosby in Paramount's *Here Comes the Groom* (1951). It had a great cast, including Jane Wyman, Alexis Smith, and Franchot Tone, with cameos by none other than Louis Armstrong, Dorothy Lamour, and Frank Fontaine, to name just a few. I got the part and worked on the film for three months. And boy, did I have the time of my life! Bing gave me a beautiful doll, which I named Dixie (after Bing's wife at the time), and Jane Wyman gave me a gorgeous dress. The movie was only a moderate box office success, but it won the Academy Award that year for Best Song, which was "In the Cool, Cool, Cool of the Evening," written by Johnny Mercer.

Jacques Gencel, Bing Crosby, and me in another scene from *Here Comes the Groom.*

Jacques Gencel (second from right), me, and our stand-ins during the making of *Here Comes the Groom*, Luz Potter (left) and Nels Nelson. Because children were allowed to work for only so many hours a day, little people were often used as our stand-ins.

James Barton and Connie Gilchrist were the talented character actors who played my grandparents in *Here Comes the Groom*. Most people don't know this, but James lost his nose in a fire many years before, so every day the makeup man had to make him an artificial one. They did a great job, too, because it looked absolutely real. The makeup man was quite busy as he also had to black out my front teeth each morning to give the effect that they were missing.

After that, I was cast in *The Greatest Show on Earth* (1952). By that time, the casting people knew me, so I usually didn't have to audition, I was just automatically cast. My director this time was the astounding Cecil B. DeMille, but again, the importance of that didn't register until years later. My part was small, but it took place under the big top, so it was just like being at a real circus. My scene was with Jimmy Stewart, who plays a clown hiding a dark secret under his funny makeup. In our scene he talks to me briefly and then gives me his dog. I was on the set for just one day, and Jimmy was very nice to me. However, I heard a different story from one of my best friends, an actress who worked with him when she was about 16.

Jimmy Stewart (left) and me in a scene from *The Greatest Show on Earth*.
I was on the set for only one day, but it was a very memorable experience.
Jimmy was wonderful to me.

She told me that Jimmy was rude and nasty and even made her cry. In one scene, she missed her cue to enter from a door and she said Jimmy just went off on her, reducing her to tears. I guess, as with everything, you can only go by your own experiences.

Case in point: Bing Crosby's sons wrote a very revealing tell-all book about him, which painted Bing in a terrible light, and yet he was absolutely wonderful when we worked together. I have a few photos that he autographed to me, and on one he wrote, "Beverly, hope to play in your next picture." Bing even sent me a Christmas card every year until he died, so I have to say that my personal experience with him was absolutely wonderful.

Funny story about Bing: I've always been extremely sensitive and emotional, and I have a tendency to cry at the drop of a hat, even to this day. Something doesn't even have to be sad to set me off; I'll cry if something is poignant, or even at the sound of a favorite song. My brother, George, used to tease me by saying, "Oh, you cry at supermarket openings," or, "Are you sure you don't have overactive tear ducts?" However, my ability to cry on cue came in very handy over the course of my career because many of the shows in which I appeared required me to shed some tears. In fact, there's a book titled "Ladies of the Western," by Boyd Majors and Michael Fitzgerald, and the chapter about me is titled "Beverly Washburn: Queen of the Criers!"

Anyway, when I was around 8 years old, Bing and Bob Hope were doing a telethon together and they invited me to come on and recite a monologue. It was a very touching piece and—surprise!—in the middle I'm supposed to start crying. Bing and Bob walked up to me (this was on live television) and Bob turned to Bing and said, "Look, Bing, real tears! Maybe I can take her with me when I have my income tax done!" The audience just roared.

Shortly after I made *The Greatest Show on Earth*, I was cast in a rather forgettable movie titled *Aaron Slick from Punkin Crick* (1952). The good part, though, was that I got to work with Dinah Shore and Alan Young, two of the nicest people ever. I don't remember a lot about the movie other than in one scene I take a bite out of Alan Young's finger! Once again, it was a fun set, but I only worked on the film for a couple of days.

Kirk Douglas and me in a scene from *The Juggler*. At the time, I had no idea how lucky I was to work with such a famous and talented actor, or to be directed by the legendary Stanley Kramer.

Another scene from *The Juggler* with me and Kirk Douglas.
Kirk was so kind and generous.

From there I was cast in *Hans Christian Anderson* (1952), starring Danny Kaye. In my big scene Danny is in jail and sings "Thumbelina" to me. I have two friends who, to this day, still prefer to call me Thumbelina rather than Beverly. *Hans Christian Anderson* was filmed at the Samuel Goldwyn Studios, and was another fun shoot. Amazingly, it's also one of those movies that a lot of people still remember me for.

Next up was *The Juggler* (1953), starring Kirk Douglas, for Columbia. They show it frequently on the classic movie channels, but surprisingly it did rather poorly during its initial release. I had a wonderful part and worked on set for several weeks. *The Juggler* was directed by Stanley Kramer and shortly after filming wrapped I received a very nice letter from him, which I still treasure, commending my acting.

I adored Kirk Douglas although, at age 8, I didn't really understand just how famous he was. Years later, as an adult, I did two episodes of *The Streets of San Francisco*, with Michael Douglas, and it was fun for me to be able to tell him that I had worked with his dad. Michael was such a terrific guy, as was Karl Malden, and it was a pleasure to work with them both.

However, shortly after, Michael left the series and was replaced by Richard Hatch. I was cast again and I couldn't get over the difference between the two. Michael was warm and friendly, whereas Richard was aloof and not very friendly. I have to say, however, that generally speaking, he was the exception. Over the years, I was lucky to work with very few people who were less than terrific.

The year I made *The Juggler*, 1953, was also the year in which I made *Shane*, starring Alan Ladd. It remains one of the best-known movies in which I appeared.

We filmed for three months in Jackson Hole, Wyoming, and then returned to the Paramount lot for a few more days of shooting. We traveled to Wyoming by train, which was a first for me. I'm not sure why they didn't just fly us there instead, but the trip took us through some gorgeous country, and it was great fun for me and my mother, who went with me.

By then I had amassed a collection of literally hundreds of dolls, and each one had a name. I wanted to take them all with me to Wyoming, but my mother told me I could take only three, so I wrote out all of their names on a piece of paper and "drew" which ones I would bring with me so as not to hurt the other's feelings. In my young mind, I figured that would be the fairest way to do it. My father couldn't come with us to Wyoming, so he told me that he would look in on all of the other dolls each day, and assured me that they would be fine until I returned home.

While in Wyoming I became very ill with a stomach flu and spent three days in the hospital. My mother was a nervous wreck because she was afraid they would replace me in the movie, but the producers were kind enough to wait for me to recover. (In my absence, they hired a local girl by the name of Gretchen Stainbrook, put her in my wardrobe, and used her to film some long shots.) When I talked to my father on the phone, I told him I would probably feel a whole lot better if perhaps one more of my "babies" could fly there to be with me. He told me that he would draw one of their names and surprise me. My only boy doll (I named him Georgie, after my brother) arrived a few days later. Guess I always was kind of a "daddy's girl." My father always spoiled me, and my mother would just smile.

I have a funny story to share about Alan Ladd. One weekend, just for the fun of it, we all took a chairlift to the top of a mountain near the location where we were filming, and Mr. Ladd was in the chair behind me. Evidently he had a severe fear of heights and when we all got to the

A group shot of the girls from *Shane*. That's me, second from the right.

top of the mountain, he refused to go back down. He was so adamant that they actually had to call a helicopter to get him!

Well, the next day on the set, the entire crew really needled him because here he was supposed to be this brave western star, and he was too terrified to ride the chairlift down. What made it worse, however, is that they all said, "Little Beverly had no problem!" At the time I was a little embarrassed that they brought me into it because I thought Mr. Ladd might be upset with me, but he took the ribbing with good humor and then gave me a hug. I was so relieved.

In the movie I played one of the Lewis children. Edgar Buchanan, who is well known to television buffs as Uncle Joe on *Petticoat Junction*, played my father and I remember him as being incredibly nice. In fact, I adored him. Unfortunately, other than the day we all rode the chairlift, I didn't really see much of Alan Ladd. I have many more fond memories of Brandon DeWilde, who played Joey Starrett, the little boy who becomes enamored with the quiet, rugged Shane. Brandon was a wonderful actor, but on set he was just like any other young boy. He used to pull all of the little girls' pigtails—mine included!

Another scene from *Shane*. That's me, sitting in front of the dresser.

Television was coming into its own during the early years of my career, and I was fortunate enough to make the transition fairly easily. I remember coming home from school one day and there in the living room was a brand new black and white TV set! It was in a blond wood console and was top of the line. Though it was rather expensive, my parents reasoned that we would need a television since I was going to be on it.

As I started appearing on television show after television show, my family suddenly acquired a new car, then new furniture, then new appliances. It never occurred to me that all of it was being paid for by me. Of course, I got a lot of nice stuff as well, such as a gorgeous canopy bed. Just like that, we went from having almost no money to being upper middle class! The money I was earning as an actress paid all the bills, though I didn't really know that for quite a long time.

One of my first television jobs was an episode of *Dragnet*, starring Jack Webb. I played a little girl who lives with her grandfather, and we get robbed. But rather than the grandfather going to the police, I do. The title of the episode was "The Big Pair." Every episode of the first *Dragnet* series was titled "the big something or other," but to this day I have no idea what "The Big Pair" means! Once, on a panel at a convention, I said, "They couldn't have been referring to me—I was only 11!" Not everyone got that joke, I might add.

Jack Webb cranked out the show week after week and didn't want to have to deal with memorizing his dialogue, so when I got on the set, I saw this contraption that was totally foreign to me—a teleprompter from which Jack read his lines. I had never seen anything like it before, and was just mesmerized. *Dragnet* fans will remember how Jack talked, in that odd, emotionless, choppy kind of way: "Just the facts, ma'am." Well, that's because he was reading his lines. But it worked for the character and he became famous for his delivery.

Jack was great to work with and I still have a wonderful autographed photo of him and his co-star, Ben Alexander. To show you what kind of man Jack was, I received a Christmas card from him every year until his death. The funny part is that the card was the same every year. It looked more like a business card, white with the embossed sign that read Mark VII, followed by "Seasons Greetings" and Jack's name. It's not the most Christmas-y card I ever received, but I was honored to be remembered by Jack every year.

Speaking of Jacks, I first worked with Jack Benny on his television show in 1952, when I was about 9 years old. That was back in the days of live television, before they even could do a tape delay. It went out to viewers as we were doing it, so there was no room for mistakes. I was "planted" in the audience, and on cue I got up from my seat and walked up on stage to ask for Jack's autograph while the guys in the orchestra pit pretended to try to stop me. Jack and I did this very long bit in which my name turns out to be Margaret Truman. At any rate, the audience loved it and thus began my life-long friendship with Jack Benny.

Jack often dropped by our house unexpectedly for a quick visit. He would pull up in his Rolls Royce and the neighbors would go crazy! He was always cordial and would wave to them and smile. As noted, ours wasn't a wealthy neighborhood, so a visit from a celebrity as famous as Jack Benny, driving a Rolls Royce, was always a thrill.

People often ask me who my favorite co-star is. I have many, but Jack and I had a very special bond. It always amused me that he played the stingy tightwad because that was as far from the real Jack Benny as you could get. He once gave me a beautiful St. Christopher necklace with the inscription: "To Beverly, with love, Jack Benny." He also gave me a gorgeous string of real pearls. When my dad was very ill in the hospital, Jack sent over his personal physician at his expense. And when I had my appendix removed, he sent a gorgeous, gigantic

Jack Benny cuts the cake during my 18th birthday party. Jack and I worked
together many times and became dear friends.

flower arrangement to the hospital, which thrilled me and the nurses as well.
Jack always remembered not only me but my parents at Christmas time, usually with a giant basket of goodies, and usually a check.

There was only one Jack Benny, that's for sure. His timing was
impeccable and his expressions were timeless. He didn't have to say a
word; he could just put his hand on his cheek and stare at the audience,
and the crowd would laugh itself into hysterics.

I later appeared on a couple of Jack's radio shows, and also appeared
with him at the Biltmore Hotel in Phoenix in a skit in which I played his

wife. (I was 9!) In addition, I worked with him at Melody Land, and appeared with him at The Hollywood Palace in another silly act in which I played one of The Smothers Sisters. (The Smothers Brothers were quite big at the time.) Iris Adrian, the wonderful character actress who often played a brassy, nasally operator, and another actress by the name of Peggy Mondo, who weighed about 300 pounds, were the other two members of the Smothers Sisters trio. We were quite a funny sight to see!

As an aside, Sammy Davis Jr. was the guest star on that particular show. He was fabulous, a remarkable talent, and one of the nicest people I've ever met. He also had a great sense of humor. Being petite, I've gotten "short" jokes my whole life, but I must say that Mr. Davis dropped one of my favorites. As he walked past me for the first time backstage, he looked at me and said, "I've got cuff links bigger than you!"

Me and Leora Dana in the "Rip Van Winkle" episode of *Shirley Temple's Storybook*.

Well, the act with Jack was a screaming success—it was so silly that the audience was just roaring—so it was decided that we would take it on the road. We played Vegas at the Sahara, then Lake Tahoe, and then we traveled all over the East Coast for six weeks. It was one of the most fun jobs I've ever had, and one of my fondest memories.

As I got to know Jack, I came to realize that deep down he was really very lonely. His wife, Mary Livingstone, never traveled with him except when we were in Vegas, and only then because she liked to gamble. I had dinner with the Benny's one night and Mary told me that Jack always gave her one hundred silver dollars with which to gamble when they were in Las Vegas.

One time when Jack and I were performing in Rhode Island we had the night off so I decided to rent a car and go visit my friend Joanie from grammar school, who lived nearby. When I returned to my hotel room after midnight, my message light was flashing. I called the operator to see who had called and she said it was Jack. I panicked because I didn't know what to do; I was afraid I would wake him because it was so late and I knew he went to bed early. I finally decided to wait until morning

Me signing autographs during a personal appearance.

since Jack hadn't left a message saying it was urgent. I called him first thing in the morning and told him that I was sorry that I hadn't called him back but I had returned quite late and I didn't want to wake him. He said he had just wanted to see if I wanted to go to a movie with him because he didn't have anybody else to go with. I've never forgotten that. I thought it was very sad and ironic. Here was one of the most famous men in the world, adored by millions, and he didn't have anyone to go to the movies with, at least in his mind, as most people would have given their right arm to be with him. As much as I liked Mary, I always thought it would

Me, Barbara Billingsley, and Lauren Chapin during an Easter brunch at the Beverly Hilton.

have been nice if she had traveled with Jack a little more.

Another time in Las Vegas, Jack's manager, Irving Fein, who was also George Burns' manager, decided to get married, so they held the wedding in Jack's penthouse suite and we were all invited, along with George. When George arrived, I thought he had brought his granddaughter or maybe a niece because the woman on his arm barely looked 21. Someone later told me that she was his date! Go George! Boy, was I naive!

Halfway through the tour, Peggy Mondo had another commitment so they flew in another actress by the name of Ida Mae McKensie. She was very talented but extremely nervous about taking over Peggy's role because Peggy had done such a great job. As we waited backstage, Ida went up to Jack and said, "Oh Mr. Benny, I'm so nervous. I haven't had much time to rehearse and I hope I do this right, I don't want to let you down" He looked at her and said "Well, Ida Mae, go out there give it your best shot and if it doesn't work…fuck it!" Well, that really broke the ice! Everyone cracked up and Ida realized she had nothing to be concerned about. We went out, did the show, and she was great. Jack, in his own inimitable fashion, had put her at ease.

Me and Jane Withers at a Hollywood-sponsored Easter brunch.
What's with my hat?!

Jack was always very sweet to me, but sometimes he could surprise you. One time, when we were playing the Sahara in Lake Tahoe, we were returning from lunch and a very inebriated man stumbled by us, turned and said in a very slurred voice, "Well, if it isn't Jack Benny!" To which Jack turned and said, "Kiss my ass!" I was flabbergasted because that was probably the last thing I ever expected to come out of Uncle Jack's mouth! It was quite funny, actually, because it was so out of character for him to say something like that, but Jack had very little tolerance for drunk people. There will never be another Jack Benny and I will be eternally grateful for his friendship.

I found early on that sometimes acting can lead to other professional relationships. For example, from the age of 10 to the
age of 12, I represented a
children's clothing company
called Debby Ross. They used my
photograph on the clothing tag
with my signature and the tag
line "You're a doll when you wear
clothes by Debby Ross." The
company didn't want me to wear
any clothes other than Debby
Ross, so every two weeks my
mother and I would go to the fac-
tory in downtown Los Angeles,
where the clothes were manufac-
tured, and I would pick out several outfits. As the company's of-
ficial representative, I also made
personal appearances at department stores that carried the line.

Me and Johnny Washbrook (*My Friend Flicka*) at an Easter brunch. Will Hutchins, the star of *Sugarfoot*, had just autographed my right hand!

I would typically model one dress, and then other girls would model others
while I sat at a table to meet the public and sign autographs. It was a lot of
fun, and I was saddened when I grew too old to continue representing the
Debby Ross line.

In 1955 I was cast in a half-hour CBS situation comedy titled *Professional Father*, starring Steve Dunne and Barbara Billingsley, who is
much better known as June Cleaver on *Leave it to Beaver*. The show
went out live every Saturday from the CBS studios in Los Angeles, com-
monly known at Television City. Other live shows produced include *The
Red Skelton Show, Playhouse 90*, and *Life with Father*. *Professional Father*
lasted only 26 weeks, but it was a great time for me.

The week before the show aired was usually quite hectic. Each Tues-
day we would have what's known as a "table read" in the rehearsal hall.
That's when the cast, the director, and the writers read through the script
together for the first time, and the director and writers would add, delete,
or change certain lines.

A cast shot from *Professional Father*, the short-lived CBS situation comedy on which I worked in 1955. Clockwise from upper left: Barbara Billingsley, Steve Dunne, me, and Ted Marc.

On Wednesday, we would return to the rehearsal hall and have a walk-through, with all of the rooms that were on the set loosely sketched on the floor with tape so we would know where to walk during each scene. On Thursday, we were back in the rehearsal hall for another walk through so the three cameramen on the show could get a feel for how each scene would look. Furniture was added for a more realistic look. On Friday, we went to the actual set and rehearsed all day with the props we would be using in each scene. In between all of this, we also had wardrobe fittings.

On Saturday, we would rehearse again, and then have a dress rehearsal to make sure everything looked okay for the camera. We'd then break for lunch, the studio audience would be ushered in, and it was time for the real thing.

I absolutely adored Barbara Billingsley and Steve Dunne. Anne O'Neill, who played Nana, and Arthur Q. Bryan, who was the handyman on the show, were also adorable. And here's a bit of trivia: Phyllis Coates, who had played Lois Lane in *Superman and the Mole Men*, played Steve Dunne' secretary/nurse on the show. It was fun working with Phyllis again, even though we hadn't had any scenes together on *Superman and the Mole Men*.

I loved working on *Professional Father*, but Ted Marc, who played my brother on the show, did not. In fact, he absolutely hated acting and was there only at the insistence of his mother. He had little acting experience but was a cute kid, so his mother had gotten him an agent, who landed him the role on *Professional Father*. When the show was canceled after one season, Ted got out of the business. We became reacquainted

Anne O'Neill (left) played Nana on *Professional Father*.
That's me in the middle, and Barbara Billingsley on the right.

about 30 years later and Ted told me again how much he had loathed show business. Today, he's a successful fencing instructor!

Live television was thrilling because there was no room for mistakes. You couldn't stop and redo a scene—if you flubbed your lines, that's what the television audience saw. However, I can remember only two incidents in which things didn't go exactly right. The first was the episode of *Lux Video Theatre* I did with Laraine Day. Laraine had a very quick wardrobe change and then she was supposed to walk in while I pretended to paint something on an easel. Well, I waited and waited, and she never walked in! Apparently the zipper on her dress had become stuck and I could see out of the corner of my eye that the wardrobe lady was frantically trying to fix it. The camera was already on me so, thinking quickly, I started ad-libbing until she came in so her delayed entrance wouldn't be so obvious. I didn't

Me and Gene Lockhart in a scene for an episode of *Schlitz Playhouse* entitled "Behind Closed Doors."

think it was a big deal, but after the show the director, the producer, and Laraine all came over, gave me a big hug, and thanked me for saving the day. I was really touched, but in my mind I was only doing my job.

The second incident occurred during the live broadcast of an episode of *Playhouse 90* on CBS. It was about a group of unwed teenagers who live together in a home, and each girl had her own little storyline. The episode starred Diane Baker, Jenny Maxwell, and another actress from New York whose name I won't reveal. I was the youngest of the group, and supposedly didn't know how I got pregnant—*duh!*—that has always amused me. At any rate, during the course of the show the New York actress was supposed to have her baby, which was, of course, a doll wrapped in a blanket.

The actress wanted to wear very high heels because she said it would help her get into character. The director protested because he felt it was too dangerous to have her walking up and down stairs in stiletto heels, and besides, her feet weren't going to be seen anyway. He told her it would be a disaster if she were to slip while the show was in progress, but she threw a tantrum and said she would be wearing high heels whether they liked it or not. They went round and round about it and she finally agreed that she would wear flats, but when the show aired live, she came walking down the stairs wearing her high heels, her "baby" wrapped in a blanket!

Jenny Maxwell and me in a scene from the episode of *Playhouse 90* in which we played unwed mothers. Amusingly, my character had no idea how she became pregnant!

Well, I'm sure you can imagine what happened next. Just as the director had predicted, she tripped on the stairs and her "baby" went flying! Needless to say, everyone gasped. The cameraman tried to cover for her by turning the camera as fast as he could, but it was pretty obvious what had happened. The actress was so shaken up that she could hardly get through the last act. Of course, the director was absolutely livid, and I don't believe that actress worked in television again for a very long time, if at all.

Funny story about that particular episode of *Playhouse 90*. When I was a child I took piano lessons for about a year. On the set of *Playhouse 90* was a piano, so one day, while we were all taking a break, I sat down, looking very pregnant thanks to a pillow under my dress, and started playing "I'm In The Mood for Love." I was only 14, so the irony of that song was lost on me, but not the crew, who started howling with laughter. I thought they were laughing at my amateurish playing, and it wasn't until one of the grips said, "Hey, nice song choice!" that I realized what I had done. After I got over my embarrassment I realized the absurdity of it all and joined in the laughter. Needless to say, I was teased about that for the rest of the show.

I did many live shows as a child but because I was blessed with a photographic memory, I never worried about forgetting my lines. Also, children tend to be more fearless than adults. I did several episodes of a show called *Matinee Theater*, which was a one-hour episodic series taped at the NBC studios in Burbank. It was on five days a week usually at noon. In one episode I played a precocious little brat who, at any given moment, would recite a lengthy poem, so not only did I have to memorize my dialogue, but I had to memorize several long poems! That was a bit of a challenge, but I like challenges, and I managed to get through the episode without missing a beat. I'm not sure I could do it again today, however.

I also appeared in an episode of *General Electric Theater*, which was hosted by Ronald Reagan. Piper Laurie played my mother, Dan Duryea played my father, and I was one of the children. We were supposed to be "mountain children" of sorts: poor, uneducated, and barefoot. However, the crew determined that it would be too dangerous for us to be walking around like that, so they fit the bottoms of our feet with moleskin which, as you can imagine, felt pretty weird.

Another weekly drama showcase in which I appeared was *Four Star Playhouse*. I did several episodes, and in one I got to work with David Niven, Charles Boyer, and Dick Powell, magnificent actors all. As I look back over my career I realize just how fortunate I was growing up to have worked with so many legends. It's sad that most of the people I've worked with are all gone now, but I guess that's all a part of life. Holding on to their memories is key. Hence, this memoir.

Because I acted in hundreds of television shows, it's sometimes difficult for me to remember some of my co-stars. I pretty much went from show to show when I was a child, enjoying the experience then moving on to the next project. For example, I appeared in an episode of *The Millionaire*, which was about a man who gives someone a million dollars and how it affects that person's life. Sadly, I don't remember much at all about the episode in which I appeared, other than the fact that my mother was played by a wonderful actress named Karen Steele. She was just beautiful and one of the sweetest ladies I ever worked with. I've often wondered what happened to her.

Telephone Time was an anthology series hosted by John Nesbitt. I auditioned for a part in an episode titled "The Man with the Beard" with the show's producer, a man named Jerry Stagg. Jerry was a rather large, gruff, menacing man, and for whatever reason I felt that he didn't like me. In fact, I was terrified of him, and for the first time in my career I actually hoped that I wouldn't get the part. I remember driving home and silently praying, "Please God, don't let me get this part!" However, I didn't tell my mother of my fears because I didn't want to disappoint her. I went to sleep that night feeling glad that the whole thing was over and I almost certainly hadn't gotten the role because it was so obvious that Jerry Stagg didn't like me. The next day, however, I came home from school to find my mother beaming because, contrary to what I had assumed, I had been cast.

This role, like so many, required me to cry. Only this time I was to cry because I had been tormented by a group of people who threw me in filth and cut off half of my hair because my father had a beard. The day of the shoot, I was sent to wardrobe and then to makeup, where they covered me in this horrible, muddy stuff so I looked like I had been thrown in a huge puddle. From there I went to the hair department. I was supposed to look like I had one side of my hair cut off and the other side was to look untouched. I had long blonde hair at the time so they parted it down the middle, then braided half and pinned it flat to the side of my head and covered it with Van Heflin's toupee to cover the hidden braid. I often wonder if Van Heflin ever knew that his toupee was worn by a 12-year-old girl on national television!

Once I was made up, I was brought to the set. Standing there (still not smiling) was Jerry Stagg. He gave me a jump rope and told me to jump until I was completely out of breath. At that point I was to let him

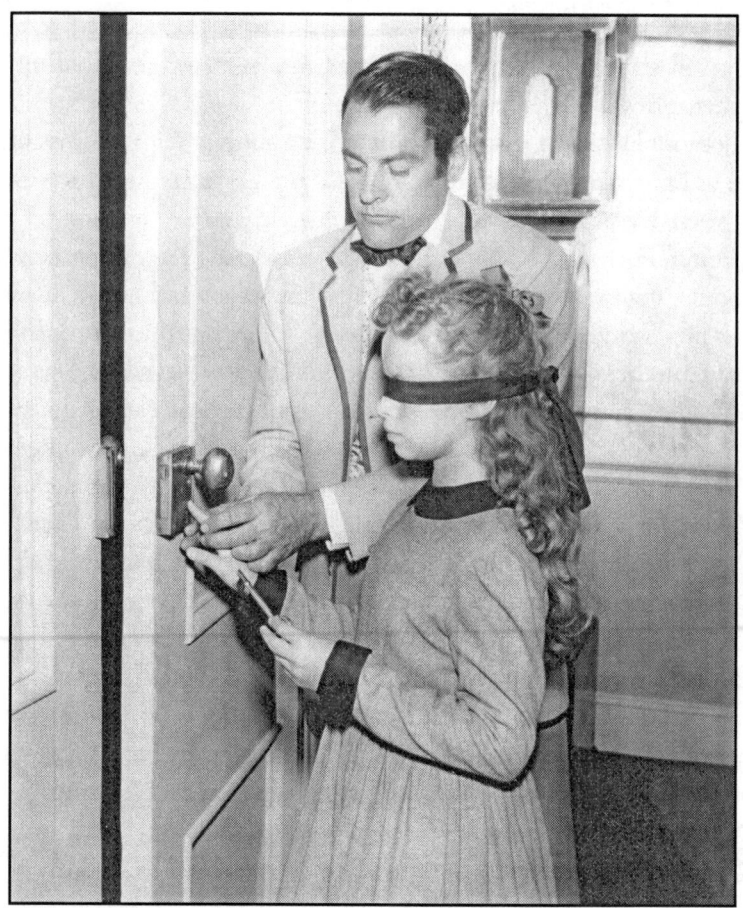

Me and Kevin McCarthy in a scene from an episode of *Telephone Time* titled "The Key." I'm wearing a blindfold because my eyes were supposedly damaged by a fever.

know I was ready and then to come in screaming, totally out of breath, do the scene and cry as hard as I could.

I decided to give it my all. After jumping rope for a few minutes, I was ready. They rolled the cameras and I came in screaming. After the scene, the director yelled "cut!" and the entire crew applauded. I looked over and there was Jerry Stagg, tears streaming down his face, crying like a baby! He then ran over to me, picked me up, and simply said, "My God!" I took that as a good sign, because I thought he was never going to stop spinning me around.

It was then that I realized that sometimes, when you think that God doesn't answer your prayers, He really does. Jerry asked my mother to bring me to his office the following week because he needed to talk to us. We dropped by as instructed and he said that he had a script that had been sitting in his office for years because he didn't think he could ever find the right child to play the part. It was a show called "The Key," and was based on a true story about a little girl named Laura Bridgeman who, years later, became one of Helen Keller's teachers. Laura supposedly had been left blind by a fever and wore a scarf tied around her eyes to hide her affliction. She also was a deaf mute who, in the show, was taught to communicate by a doctor played by Kevin McCarthy. Jerry told me that when an actor can't communicate by words, she must use her eyes to express herself. This role, he explained, would be extremely difficult because I wouldn't be able to talk OR use my eyes to express myself, since I would have a scarf wrapped around my head, covering

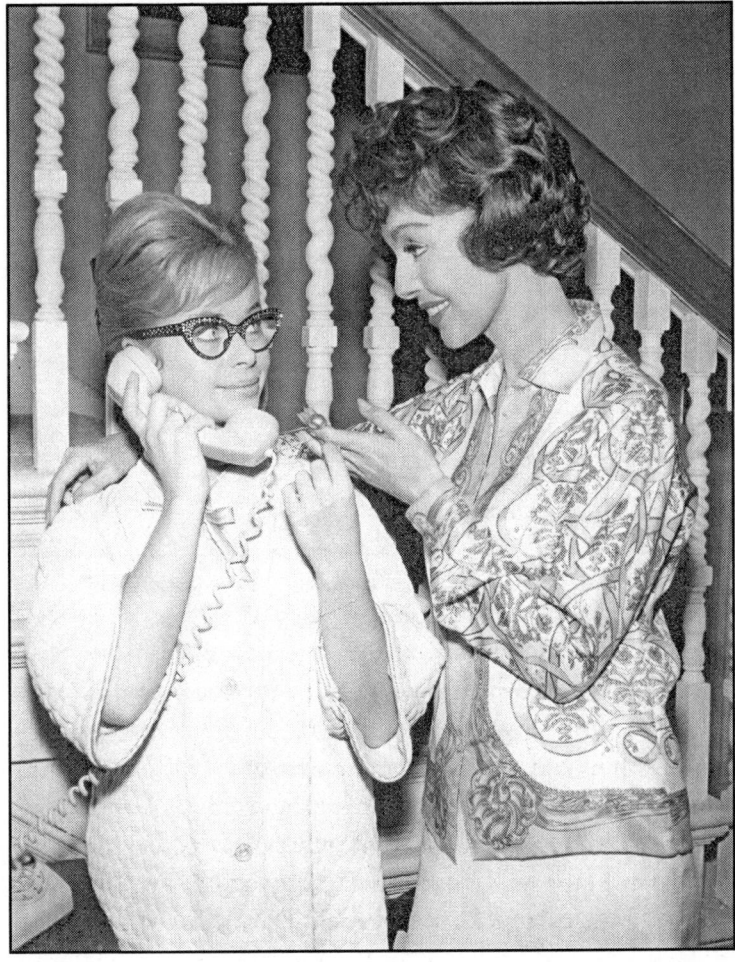

Me and my dear friend Loretta Young in a scene from *The New Loretta Young Show*.
I played the family bookworm.

A cast shot from *The New Loretta Young Show*. That's me in the glasses on the left.

my eyes. He said he hadn't produced the script because he hadn't been able to find a young actress capable of doing it justice, then he looked at me and said, "Now I know I have." I was deeply touched.

I did the show and it was for that performance that I was nominated for an Emmy. I also consider it one of the highlights of my acting career. After the shoot was over, Jerry gave me a beautiful engraved bracelet with a tiny key to represent the show. That was the beginning of a long friendship with Jerry, which continued until he passed away. I also loved working with Kevin McCarthy; he was an incredible actor and very kind man. I still have a signed photo from him that says, "To Beverly: A consummate actress." I feel honored to have had the privilege of working with him. Of course, at 12 I didn't know what "consummate" meant. I thought he meant constipated!

In the mid 1950s I appeared in four episodes of *The Loretta Young Show*, also known as *Letter to Loretta*. It lasted just two seasons, but working with Loretta, who defined the concept of movie star, was a tremendous thrill.

Several years later, when I was 19, Loretta called me to say that she was going to be doing a new television series and that she would like me to play one of her daughters (the homely, intellectual one). It was called *The New Loretta Young Show*, and Loretta played a widow with seven children. Dirk and Dack Rambo (real names: Orman and Norman) played the twin boys on the show. They were both gay, although no one knew it at the time. In real life they had a sister named Beverly and her nickname was Bonzo, so they took it upon themselves to call me Little Bonzo, which was a name that stuck for as long as I knew them. Sadly, Dirk was killed in an automobile accident and burnt beyond recognition, the result of a drunk driver who plowed into his car while driving on the wrong side of the street. Dack did quite a bit of television work, but he eventually died of AIDS. They were two of the sweetest guys I've ever known.

Loretta's niece, Betty Jane, who was nicknamed BJ, had a huge crush on Dirk and I had a huge crush on Dack. Because they were gay, nothing came of it, but we still had some great times together. One year the four of us went to the Academy Awards and got to walk down the red carpet, which was a tremendous thrill.

When the show was first cast, the first actress to land a role was Portland Mason, James Mason's daughter. Next was Carol Sydes, who later changed her name to Cindy Carol. Cindy was later cast as Gidget in *Gidget Goes to Rome* (1963). The third girl was Sandy Descher, followed by Tracy Stratford. We had one rehearsal and the next day there was no Portland Mason! We were never really told what had happened, but suddenly Portland had been replaced by Celia Kaye.

I was chosen by the network to be the representative for the show on a national press junket. It was a whirlwind two-week tour in which reps from all of CBS's new series flew around the country to plug their shows on various regional TV and radio shows. I never knew why I was selected to promote *The New Loretta Young Show*, but I was very grateful for the opportunity, which proved to be a fabulous experience. Unfortunately, all of my hard work was for naught. *The New Loretta Young Show* ran for just one season, killed in the ratings by *Ben Casey*, which was the hottest show on television at the time.

Over the years, I lost touch with Loretta; not for any particular reason, but rather because things change. However, I never forgot about her because she had been one of the most influential people in my career, and I loved her very much.

One day while talking to my friend, Rick Saphire, Loretta's name came up and Rick said to me how sad it was that she had died so long ago. I told him that I was sure she was still alive, and that I would have heard if she had passed away. But Rick was adamant that Loretta was gone, so I told him I would dig up her old phone number and try to track her down, even though we hadn't seen each other in years.

I was nervous about making the call and prayed that she was still alive, as I knew I would be devastated if she had died and I hadn't known. Loretta's housekeeper answered the phone, I told her who I was, and the next thing I knew I was talking to Loretta herself! Of course, I didn't tell her about the premature rumors of her death, only that I called because I had been thinking of her. We had a lovely conversation and I was so thrilled that we were back in touch after all these years. My husband, Mike, had been diagnosed with cancer, and we talked about that at length. A few days later I received in the mail a little book about angels with a note from Loretta telling me that she would keep Mike in her prayers. After that, we spoke about once a week, which was an absolute pleasure. She continued to send me little gifts, including a little stained-glass dove and a beautiful green scarf, for no reason other than to say she was thinking of me. Needless to say, I was deeply touched. That's how Loretta was: caring, loyal, generous, and very sweet. To this day, I realize how truly blessed I am to have known such an incredible person.

One day, while we were talking, I said to Loretta, "You're such a legend and people love you so much. Would you ever consider doing a film again?" She said, "You know, honey, I get scripts sent to me almost daily, but they're not the kind of stories I would want to do. There's too much sex and violence and bad language, and they're just not appealing to me." There was a pause, then she added, "Besides, I'm too old, too tired…and too rich." And then she started laughing. It was so out of character to hear her laughing at herself like that, but it was adorable and I'll never forget it. We continued to talk for about a year, and she invited Mike and me to come and stay in her guest house in Palm Springs. Unfortunately, we never took her up on her generous invitation, which I deeply regret. Shortly after, Loretta's health started to decline, and I could hear in her voice that she was getting tired. When she finally passed away, I cried for a very long

The wonderful Anne Baxter and me in a scene from an episode of
Zane Grey Theater titled "Stars Over Texas."

time. I learned then that you should never put off something that's important to you because the opportunity may never come again.

A couple of years after Loretta died, I was tracked down by her son,
Christopher. They decided to put the entire series we had done together
on DVD and rename it *Christine's Children*. Christopher came to my
house and videotaped me talking about Loretta, and our conversation is
included on the DVD. Though I wasn't compensated for the interview
or for the DVD sales, I was happy to be a part of it as Loretta was one of
my favorite people in the world.

In 1956, I got a call to go on an audition for the feature film *The
Lone Ranger*, starring Clayton Moore, Jay Silverheels, and Bonita
Granville. I was getting a little spoiled by not having to audition but I
hadn't yet worked at Warner Brothers, which was producing the movie,

FIRST TIME ON THE BIG, WIDE, MOTION PICTURE SCREEN!

"The Lone Ranger" and Tonto too!!!

a JACK WRATHER production presented by WARNER BROS. in WARNERCOLOR

A lobby card from the movie version of *The Lone Ranger*, starring Clayton Moore and Jay Silverheels. That's Bonita Granville behind me.

so they wanted me to come in and read. I was excited because I was enthralled with *The Lone Ranger*. I was now 12 and was feeling very comfortable in front of the camera, so I wasn't nervous, just excited.

When I arrived for the audition, the waiting room was filled with many other hopefuls. My mother gave me her usual encouraging speech, noting, "Just do your best, honey, and if it's meant to be then you'll get the part. But if you don't, then don't be sad because something else will come along." Looking back, I think that was what was so wonderful about my mother in regard to my acting career—she was always very supportive, encouraging me every step of the way, but she never pushed me. A lot of the stage parents we saw on auditions became angry if their children didn't get a part, but my mother always maintained a positive attitude, and that rubbed off on me.

The very next day my agent called to tell us that I had gotten the part. I was so grateful and thrilled to be in yet another film. Most of the filming was done in Kanab, Utah. We worked for three months and it was wonderful. Kanab is such a beautiful, spiritual place.

Me during a wardrobe test for *The Lone Ranger*. I was quite the little cowgirl!

The shoot was pretty uneventful, and we all had a good time. In one scene I get kidnapped by some Indians and, of course, the Lone Ranger comes to my rescue. We were out on location and Clayton Moore was in his very tight costume. As he jumped up on Silver to ride away, his pants split totally open and his bare butt popped out, only Clayton didn't know it. The director decided to let the camera keep rolling as a joke so that later they could show it in the outtakes. As a result, the running joke on the set became: *As the Lone Ranger was riding off into the sunset, he was mooning everyone!* Clayton was a great sport about it, and everyone got a good laugh. I was young so I was a little embarrassed, but I couldn't help but laugh because it really was funny.

Me with Arthur Franz in an episode of *Science Fiction Theater* entitled "The Strange People at Pecos." Sadly, I can't remember the name of the actress with us.

An eerie shot from an episode of *Thriller* titled "Parasite Mansion," starring Jeanette Nolan and Pippa Scott. The greatest thrill for me was meeting the show's host, Boris Karloff!

It was in Clayton's contract that he would never be photographed without his famous mask. One Sunday, while we were all enjoying a day off in the hotel pool, a female fan recognized him and asked if he would pose for a picture with her. Clayton quickly grabbed his mask and struck a pose. I immediately started giggling because it was so comical to see the Lone Ranger wearing nothing but swimming trunks and a mask!

After filming in Utah for three months, we returned to the studio to finish up. I had come to love the cast and crew, and it was extremely difficult saying goodbye to them all because they had become like family to

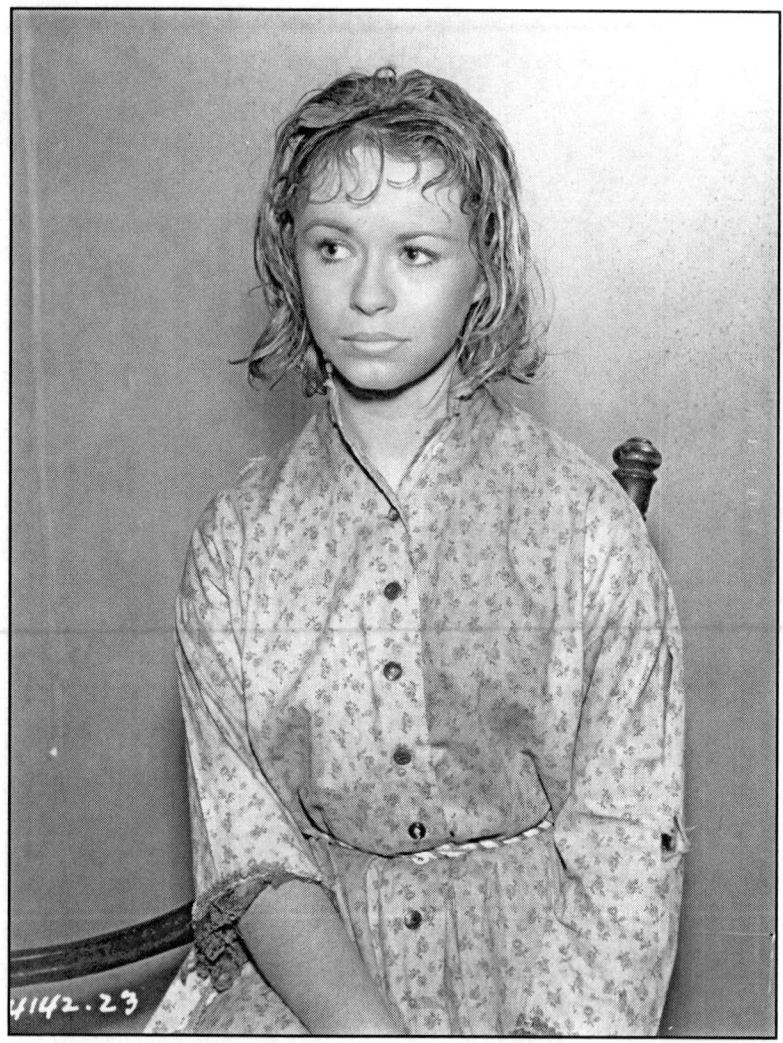

Me on the set of "Parasite Mansion," a really fun episode of *Thriller*.

me. As for Clayton Moore—he'll always be the Lone Ranger in my heart. And of course, Jay Silverheels, who portrayed Tonto, was wonderful.

Over the course of my career I have appeared in a number of science fiction and horror television shows and movies. One of the most memorable for me was an anthology series called *Thriller*, hosted by the inimitable Boris Karloff.

The episode in which I appeared was called "Parasite Mansion," and it was one of my favorite roles. Jeanette Nolan, who was a marvelous actress, played my grandmother, a witch who locked me in my room and caused horrible things to happen to me. Pippa Scott (the other guest star) stumbles upon the house when her car breaks down in a storm and finds me locked up in the attic.

I vividly remember a scene in which we're at the dinner table and all of a sudden I scream and clutch my face, revealing claw marks caused by the witch! The effect was created by gluing a small sponge to the palm of my hand, cutting three ridges down the sponge and applying Hershey's chocolate syrup on each ridge. During the scene I had my hand palm down so you couldn't see anything and then on cue I screamed, put my hand to my face and voila—the three ridges of "blood" were transferred to my cheek. It was a wonderful role.

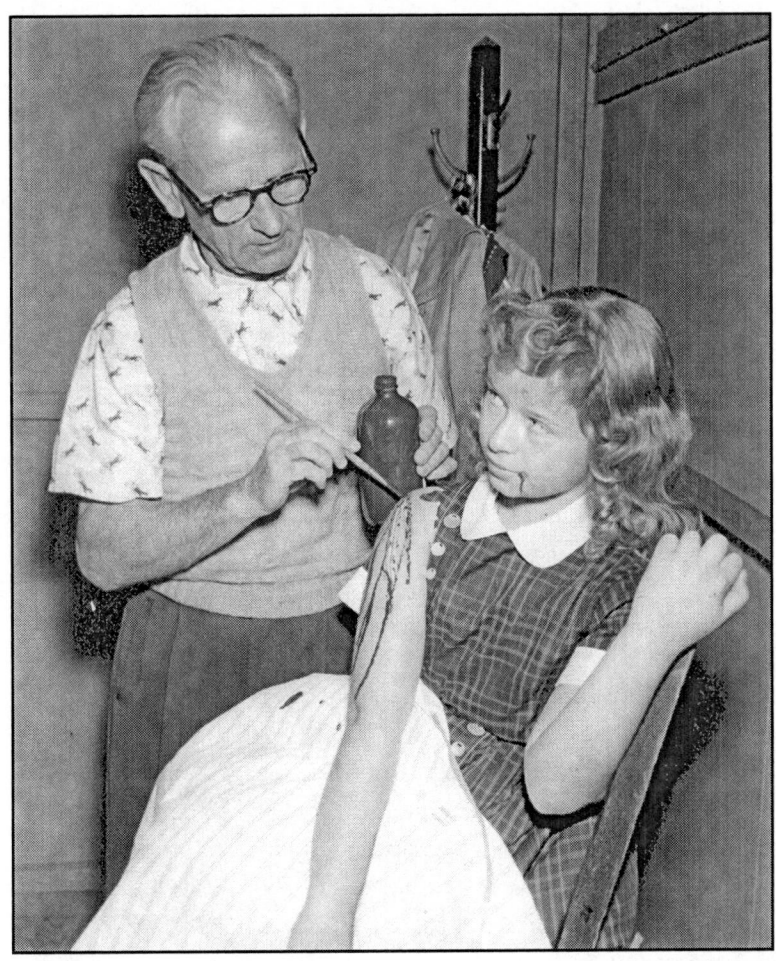

A makeup man applies chocolate syrup as fake blood for an episode of *Science Fiction Theater* titled "The Strange People at Pecos."

There was another great scene in which we're sitting at the dining room table and suddenly a tin cup raises up from the table and starts pounding me on the head, all of which is supposed to have been caused by my grandmother. They achieved that effect by attaching the cup to some fishing line and having a prop man stand on a ladder with the pole. Then, on cue, he started pounding me on the head—and he got paid to do that!

I loved doing *Thriller* because I was (and still am) a big fan of Boris Karloff. He wasn't in the episode, but he was on the set and in the beginning of the show, the camera panned around to each of us as he introduced us one by one. I was in total awe of him.

That job was fun because I also got to go next door where they were filming *Leave It to Beaver*. I had a great excuse to be there because Barbara Billingsley had played my mother many years earlier in *Professional Father*.

Me clinging to Dorothy McGuire in a dramatic moment from *Old Yeller*.

At that time, I (and every other teenage girl in America) had a huge crush on Tony Dow, so I was thrilled to get to meet him. Here I was, about to meet my future husband!...okay, that didn't happen. *But I could dream, couldn't I?* That was the beginning of a life-long friendship that continues to this day. I later got to appear in an episode of *Leave It to Beaver* titled "The Blind Date Committee," in which Wally is in charge of blind dates and can't get anyone to go out with me, so he gets stuck with me. Not surprisingly, Tony and I did a lot of "phony" dating for the fan magazines. But even though we were never romantically in-volved, a date with Tony was al-ways a lot of fun.

My "Box Office Blue Ribbon Award" for *Old Yeller*, selected Best Picture of the Month for February 1958.

One Step Beyond was another interesting horror anthology show, and one of my favorites because of director John Newland, with whom I had worked a few years earlier on *The Loretta Young Show*. The episode in which I co-starred was called "Premonition," and in it I played a little girl who, while dancing under a huge crystal chandelier, has a premonition that it falls on her. Of course, years later as an adult, the premonition comes true.

During the filming of that episode my father was in the hospital and had to have a kidney removed. Back then, it was a far more dangerous procedure than it is today. I was very distraught over the timing, but my father made me promise to work on the show, motivating me with the classic adage: "The show must go on!" I was about 15 at the time and I wrestled with that concept because I adored acting, but my father was the most important thing in the world to me. I finally decided that I didn't want to work on that episode, but my father convinced me that he would be fine and that he couldn't wait to see me on the show when it aired. I finally decided to go ahead with the filming, although my heart wasn't completely in it. Fortunately, everything went well with my father's surgery and after three weeks, he was able to come home from the hospital.

One of the movies for which I'm best known to the public is Walt Disney's *Old Yeller*, which I made in 1957. I auditioned for the role of Lisbeth, and being the huge animal lover that I am, I REALLY wanted the part. I feel very fortunate because there were several Mouseketeers who could have gotten the part just easily as I did. Old Yeller, whose real name was Spike, had been rescued from an animal shelter and was trained by the famous Weatherwax family. He was a great dog and if I remember correctly, his dressing room was bigger than mine!

Here's an interesting tidbit: The little puppy that was supposed to be Old Yeller's offspring had to go into makeup each day to be powdered down so that he would be the exact color as Old Yeller. I remember going into the makeup room and seeing the puppy sitting in the makeup chair, looking so cute. I also remember that they put a little chicken-flavored

Me and Kevin Corcoran on the set of *Old Yeller*.

Kevin Corcoran, Jeff York, and me in a touching moment from *Old Yeller*.
The puppy that played Old Yeller's offspring had to have special makeup
so he'd be the same color as his daddy.

baby food on my neck to get him to kiss me.

I developed a huge crush on Tommy Kirk while making *Old Yeller*, and we went "steady" during the filming. Tommy gave me a very "romantic" skull and cross bones ring.

Working at the Disney Studio was really interesting because the lot had street names such as Dopey Drive and Minnie Avenue. It was kept very pristine, almost a park-like setting. School was held in a big red trailer on the lot and I attended with all the Mouseketeers, several of whom I'm still friends with today.

I was thrilled to meet Walt Disney while making that movie. He would visit the set periodically and I remember him as being very nice and

Me and Tommy Kirk in a scene from *Old Yeller*. Tommy and I "dated"
briefly during the making of the film.

very soft spoken. Unlike Loretta Young, who had her hand in everything,
Mr. Disney didn't say much and let everyone do their job. Of course, he
had the final say as to me being cast, and for that I am truly grateful.

I received a wonderful letter after the filming of *Old Yeller* from
Fred Gibson, the author of the book upon which the movie was based,
thanking me for my performance and complimenting me on my accent.
I was truly honored.

Also in 1957, I made my first of three appearances in *Wagon Train*,
one of television's most popular westerns. The episode was titled "The
Willy Moran Story," and I co-starred with Ernest Borgnine, who was
marvelous. I recently ran into Ernest at an autograph show, and I must
say that he remains one of the nicest people in the business. He had a line
of people waiting for his autograph that went on forever, and he sat at his
table and signed photo after photo without complaint. He never hesi-
tated to shake a fan's hand, offer a hug, or pose for a photograph—and he
was 90 years old! Ernest truly is an inspiration.

In my second appearance on *Wagon Train*, "The Tobias Jones Story,"
I co-starred with the inimitable Lou Costello. This was Lou's first (and
only) dramatic role, and I was very excited because I was a huge fan of

Abbott and Costello. I didn't know what to expect, but it turned into one of the best experiences of my life.

Lou was incredible, and we got along as if we had known each other our entire lives. However, he had a difficult time memorizing his lines because he was used to playing fast and loose with dialogue and ad-libbing quite a bit. Every time he would forget a line, rather than just continuing he would turn to the camera and say, "So, how are ya?", which made the whole crew laugh.

In one scene, I was supposed to help Lou into a wagon. We rehearsed it all manner of ways, but it proved difficult because Lou was so much larger than I was. Finally, he turned to me and said, "Honey, I'm going to lean back and you just give me a shove on my biscuits and push me in." I just got silly laughing because I had never heard that expression before.

Me and Lou Costello in an episode of *Wagon Train* entitled "The Tobias Jones Story."

In that episode, I played an orphan who is befriended by Lou's character, Tobias Jones. We stow away on the wagon train, and Tobias is later accused of a murder he didn't commit. The others want to hang him, but—surprise, surprise—I have a big crying scene because I know he couldn't have done it. That episode, which was written by Harry von Zell, goes to show you how times have changed. Back then, in 1958, no one thought twice about a show in which a little girl travels with a man to whom she is not related. Today, such an idea would be considered very inappropriate.

Several months after we worked together, Lou published his autobiography. In it, he discussed that episode of *Wagon Train*, and was extremely kind toward me, saying that if it hadn't been for me, he couldn't

Me and Molly Bee in a scene from *Summer Love*.
Molly was so much fun to work with.

Me and George "Foghorn" Winslow do some laundry in *Summer Love*.

have done it. I was touched by his words, and honored to have been able to work with him. In my opinion, he did a marvelous job.

I also have fond memories of working with Ward Bond on *Wagon Train*. He was incredibly nice and made me feel very welcome. He autographed a photo for me, which still hangs on my wall, inscribed: "To Beverly, the finest little actress."

It should be noted that Ward had a really foul mouth. He didn't mean to swear in front of me, but he was so used to being around a bunch of guys that it just came rolling out. His cussing didn't really bother me, but it made my welfare worker furious, and at one point she told the director that if Ward used one more swear word in front of me, she was going to yank me off the set. They explained the situation to Ward, who apologized and never said so much as "darn" after that.

In 1958, I made a movie for Universal titled *Summer Love*, with John Saxon, Troy Donahue, John Wilder, Jill St. John, Judi Meredith, Shelley Fabares, and Molly Bee. Molly and I played sisters, and she was great. Each of us was kind of paired off. I was supposed to be the youngest and I played many of my scenes opposite a young actor named George "Foghorn" Winslow,

Fun times at the Santa Claus Lane Parade in Hollywood! That's me bottom left, with Lassie, Tommy Rettig (*Lassie*), Sherry Jackson (*The Danny Thomas Show*), and Santa himself!

whose credits include *Gentlemen Prefer Blondes* (1953) and *Artists and Models* (1955). There's a scene in *Summer Love* in which George and I are supposed to do the laundry for the older group of kids. (We were about 14 and everyone else was about 18, except for Shelley, who is actually my age but was playing older in the movie.) We put too much starch in the water and there's a silly scene in which we make a pair of men's long johns sit upright.

We filmed most of the movie in Lake Arrowhead, California, and we all got along wonderfully. John Wilder was almost like my big brother, and years later, when he became the producer of *The Streets of San Francisco*, he kindly cast me in three episodes.

A few years ago, I was doing an autograph signing and learned that Troy Donahue was going to be there. I was sure he wouldn't remember me because we didn't have any scenes together, but when I went up to him and introduced myself, he gave me a big hug and said, "Whatever happened to that movie? I can't find it anywhere!" Troy didn't do many autograph shows, but the next day I was at my table and a fan came over to me and said, "Some of the actors I've met seem to be a little full of themselves, but I just met Troy Donahue and he was so nice. I've decided that you and Troy are now my two favorites as you're both so friendly and you take the time to talk to us, as well as sign autographs." I thanked her and said, "Let's go over to Troy." At his table, I said, "Troy, this lady just told me that you and I are her two favorite people at this show so I brought her back here." With that,

A scene from my one and only appearance on *Father Knows Best*. That's Elinor Donahue on the left, and my dear friend Lauren Chapin in the middle.

he got up, walked around the table, and gave her a big hug and kiss on the cheek! I thought she was going to faint! I really admired Troy for doing that because he made her day. He couldn't have been nicer, and I was so happy that our paths had crossed again after all those years. A week later, I read that he had died. I had no idea it would affect me so much, but I was deeply saddened by his death. Troy was one heck of a guy.

In 1961 I was cast in an episode of a short-lived television show called *Ichabod and Me*, starring George Chandler and Robert Sterling. I played a teenager who gets engaged and returns to her parents' house with her fiancé. I can't recall the name of the actor who played my soon-to-be husband, though I do remember that he was very nice.

I have no idea why the casting director put the two of us together, though, because my co-star was about 6-foot-4 and I'm barely 5 feet tall! In the scene in which we show up together on my parents' doorstep, they open the door and see us standing there. The only problem was that, because of the huge difference in our heights, the cinematographer couldn't fit both of us in the shot. They either got his face and my eyebrows to the top of my head, or my face and his chest! It posed a hilarious dilemma and the crew got a big kick out of it. After trying various angles without success, they finally brought in an apple box for me to stand on for the entire scene. This wasn't the first time I've had to stand on a box because of my diminutive stature, but this time it was a REALLY BIG apple box!

A publicity shot of me and Bobby Rydell taken for *Teen Magazine*.

Among the many television series I did during the 1960s was a very popular detective show called *77 Sunset Strip*, starring Efrem

At a party with Dirk and Dack Rambo, who co-starred with me in *The New Loretta Young Show,* and Annette Funicello.

Me and Johnny Crawford, who starred with Chuck Connors in *The Rifleman,* at a publicity function.

Bill Bixby was my escort during the 1964 Deb Star Ball at the Hollywood Palladium.

A group shot of all of the participants of the Twelfth Annual Deb Star Ball at the Holly-wood Palladium. That's me seated on the left. Also participating that year were Raquel Welch (standing, fourth from right); Mary Ann Mobley, Miss America 1959 (second from left); and Barbara Parkins, who starred in *Valley of the Dolls* (third from right).

My formal portrait for the 1964 Deb Star Ball.

Zimbalist, Jr. In one scene I was supposed to come out of a house while talking with Mr. Zimbalist. We rehearsed the scene twice, and as we did so I was chewing gum (something I no longer do.) When we were ready to shoot, I decided that I didn't want to get rid of my gum because it was a relatively short scene, so I hid it in the palm of my hand. Well, the camera rolled, we walked out of the fake house door and for the first time, Mr. Zimbalist took my hand, which he had not done during rehearsal. Suddenly my gum was now in his palm! I was beyond mortified and couldn't stop apologizing. Luckily, he thought it was pretty funny and was very sweet about it, but I was totally embarrassed. Needless to say, that was the last time I ever chewed gum while working.

I've worked with many, many wonderful performers over the years, and one of my favorites was Patty Duke. I was a guest on her show in 1965, playing one of her girlfriends, and we found out she and I are exactly the same size. I remember walking into the wardrobe department when Patty and I first met. She introduced herself to me and welcomed me. The wardrobe lady told her she was trying to find something for me to wear when Patty spoke up and said, "Hell, looks like we're about the same size, just give her something of mine to wear!" I was flabbergasted! I couldn't believe that such a famous actress actually didn't mind if I wore a piece of her wardrobe. That's when I knew that Patty Duke was a wonderful, down to earth person.

So was Sally Field, with whom I worked on two episodes of *Gidget*. Sally's stepfather was Jock Mahoney, who very kindly helped me get into the business. One of the episodes of *Gidget* in which I appeared was about a slumber party, and I played one of Gidget's girlfriends. Two other girls at the party were played by Bonnie Franklin, who is best remembered for the television series *One Day at a Time*, and the wonderful Barbara Hershey.

In my second episode of *Gidget*, I played Paul Lynde's daughter. It was titled "Take a Lesson," and Gidget and my character get their driver's licenses. Paul Lynde was hilarious, and spoke in real life exactly as he did on screen! Until then, I had always thought his persona was just an act, but it wasn't. We laughed nonstop.

Also terrific was Lauren Chapin, with whom I worked on *Father Knows Best*. I played a poor girl whom Lauren's character, Kathy, befriends during a spelling bee. She and I got along famously, but lost touch with each other, and it wasn't until many years later that Lauren and I became such good friends. To this day, her children call me Aunt Beverly.

At that time in the 1960s, fan magazines were very popular and I found myself in most of them on a steady basis. A network or movie studio publicity department would set up "dates" between popular male and female actors, and we would go to various functions and be photographed as though we were on a real date.

These set-ups were great fun for me because I got to go on "dates" with a variety of popular (and handsome) teen actors such as Tony Dow, Paul Petersen, Tommy Kirk, Eddie Hodges, Bobby Rydell, Johnny Crawford, and Don Grady, just to name a few. And even though nothing romantic ever developed, I have remained good friends with all of them. Sadly, I was never fixed up with either of the Everly Brothers, which is a shame because I could have ended up as Beverly Everly!

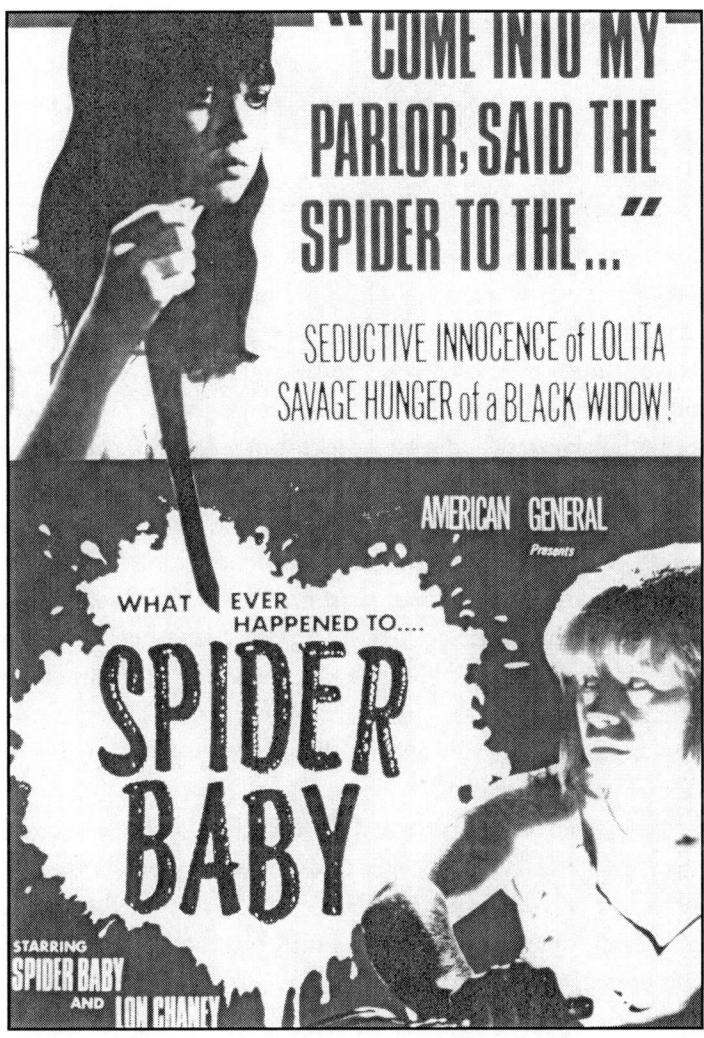

The poster for *Spider Baby*, one of my most popular movies.

Back in the day they had something called The Deb Star Ball. It was held at the Palladium in Hollywood and was televised. It was sponsored by the makeup and hair departments of the major studios and they would nominate ten girls who they thought would achieve stardom. It wasn't really a beauty contest, or a contest of any kind, just ten girls who would be introduced on stage and asked one question. Each girl who was nominated had to have a sponsor; it could be a studio, a producer, a celebrity or a specific production. (When I was nominated, my sponsor was Jack Benny.) Then each girl was given an escort. Mine was Bill Bixby. As we were rehearsing to walk out on stage, at which time each escort presented his girl with a long-stemmed red rose, Bill told me that he was near-sighted and would have a hard time seeing the cue cards, so he asked me to help him out. I laughed and said that I was about to ask him the same thing! Bill said that we would have to hold onto each other tightly as we were walking so that neither of us would miss any steps. I thought to myself, "Wow, I don't mind that at all!"

After the show, Bill took me out to a very nice restaurant on the Sunset Strip. He was wonderful, adorable, and I just fell in love. Nothing really came of our relationship, however, except another wonderful memory.

Back in the 60's, when I was regularly appearing in all of the movie magazines, it was common for popular teen stars to cut a record. For example, Shelley Fabares had a hit with "Johnny Angel," and Paul Petersen also had a hit record. I got a call from the William Morris Agency, which represented me at the time, saying that they had a recording contract for me. I was so excited, except for one problem: I don't sing! I told my agent that, there was a beat, and then he asked, "Well, can you carry a tune?" I said yes, and my agent said, "Okay, then there's no problem." And the next thing I knew, I was in the recording studio with back-up singers and a full orchestra, singing my heart out! The producers also used echo chambers to give the song that "bubble gum" quality that was so popular at the time.

The song I recorded was titled "Everybody Loves Saturday Night," written by the legendary Pete Seeger, and it was on the Smash label, which was a subsidiary of Mercury Records. Believe it or not, the song actually made the charts! It never made number one, but the fact it made the charts at all, considering all of the competition, always made me proud.

I hadn't thought about the record for decades, but it all came back to me when I recently learned that it had been included on a double CD titled "Growin' Up Too Fast: The Girl Group Anthology." Also featured on the collection are Dusty Springfield, Lesley Gore, and Connie Francis, among others. I was stunned to learn about its existence because no one contacted me about it, nor was I compensated for the inclusion of my song. Perhaps the producers thought I was dead, or maybe they just decided to chance that I'd never find out about it. Sadly, that happens a lot.

In 1968 I made what remains the most unusual movie of my career, a twisted little horror movie titled *Spider Baby*. It was about a family of cannibals (the shooting title was *Cannibal Orgy, or The Maddest Story Ever Told*), and I played Elizabeth, one of the daughters.

Me, Mary Mitchel and Quinn Redecker in a scene from *Spider Baby*.

Caption: Me and Jill Banner vamp it up in a scene from *Spider Baby*.

A touching scene from *Spider Baby*. Left to right: me, Sid Haig, Jill Banner, and the inimitable Lon Chaney Jr.

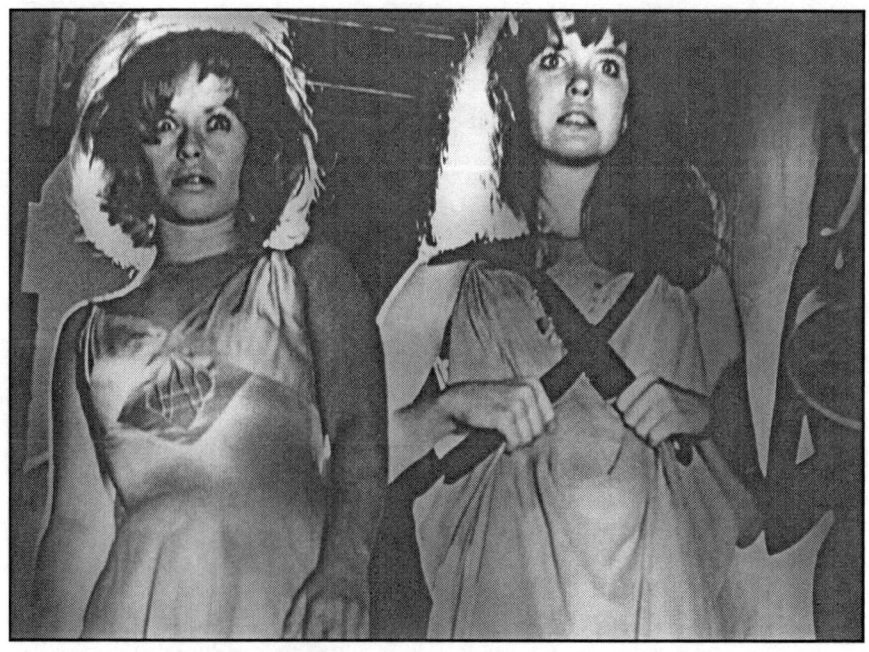

Me (left) and Jill Banner in a chilling scene from *Spider Baby*. We both look like we could use some decaf!

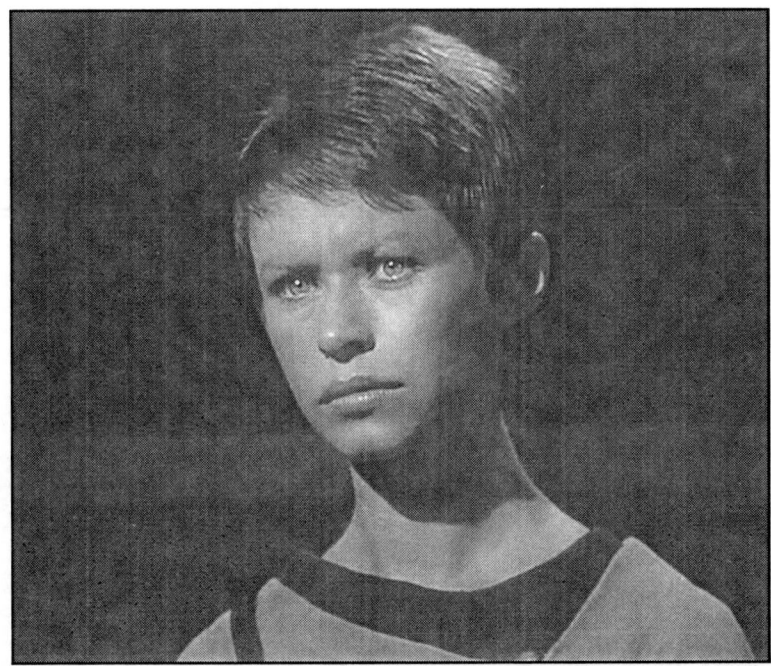

Me as Lt. Arlene Galway in "The Deadly Years," my sole appearance on *Star Trek*.
Even though my character dies of old age, appearing in *Star Trek* was the
experience of a lifetime.

knew I had landed the role. I never knew if they liked my reading or if they just
needed someone who would go along with that procedure! It took about four
and a half hours to do my makeup. When fans ask me now how long it took, I
like to tease them by saying "about the same time as it does now!"

It was great fun and I feel incredibly blessed to have been a part of
such a huge global phenomenon. There are no greater fans than *Star
Trek* fans, although horror and western fans run a close second! Although
I had only a small part in *Star Trek*, I'm forever amazed at how the fans
remember me and my character. Sometimes they will even say my line:
"That's a stupid place to hang a mirror!" I died of old age in the episode.
Hmm, I died and I wasn't even wearing a red shirt!

Some people who remember me as having long, blond hair as both a
child and an adult are curious as to why I happened to have such short,
dark hair in *Star Trek*. Well, just before I got the part I had made *Pit Stop*.
In that movie I played opposite a wonderful actor by the name of Dick
Davalos, who also appeared in *East of Eden* (1955) with James Dean. Dick
and I had the same color hair and Jack Hill thought it would look better if

My big death scene in "The Deadly Years." That episode remains a favorite
among *Star Trek* fans.

we didn't, so he asked me to change mine. I said that would be fine and I
was sent to have my hair dyed. Well, as soon as they got done dyeing my
hair, it all fell out!! They had no choice but to cut it extremely short in what
they called a "pixie" cut. So that's why my hair was like that in *Star Trek*. It
gradually grew out and then I went back to being blonde.

One of my big claims to fame is that I appear in the famous (and
infamous) *Star Trek* blooper reel, which has been making the rounds at
Star Trek conventions for almost 40 years. As an actress, I always try to
come prepared, know my lines, be on time, etc., but that was such a fun
set and the cast and crew were so great that when I blew my line, everyone cracked up. I had no idea that my gaffe would make it to the blooper
reel, or would actually be released on video. I've attended a lot of conventions where the fans will bring that up and we always have a good
laugh over it. All wonderful memories for me.

It was great working with William Shatner, Leonard Nimoy and the
whole cast, though I didn't have that much interaction with them. I remember Leonard Nimoy as being a lot more reserved and quieter than

William Shatner. In fact, Bill was quite the cut-up, especially when they put the gray in his hair as he was starting to age. When I walked into the makeup room, I didn't recognize him because he was almost totally bald! They were putting on his toupee when I walked in. He didn't say anything about it, although I don't think everyone knew, including me.

In the years that followed, I appeared in a number of television series, including *Getting Together*, *The Manhunter*, *The Streets of San Francisco*, *Disneyland* (also known as *Disney's Wonderful World*), *Scarecrow and Mrs. King*, *Las Vegas*, and many, many more. (To learn more about my career and the many movies and television shows in which I appeared, please visit my website: http://ricksaphire.com/bev/). All were great fun, and I was happy to keep my hand in acting. It's all I've ever wanted to do, and I hope to continue acting to the very end.

Me and the remarkable Barbara Stanwyck in a scene from the pilot of a proposed series titled *Calhoun*. The series didn't sell, so they turned it into a Movie of the Week.

Part Three

Then and Now

My most prolific period as an actress was childhood.

I worked almost constantly in both movies and television, and it seemed as if the good life would last forever. But as is often the case in Hollywood, as I grew older job opportunities became less frequent. I continued to work throughout my teenage years, but not as often as I did when I was younger.

I lived at home with my parents through my late teens and into my 20s, and remained my family's primary breadwinner during that time. My father's health continued to decline and he started to develop diabetic sores on his feet. He could no longer work, and my mother had never worked, but luckily I was able to get enough acting gigs to still support them and pay for our big white house.

When I was 20, my father returned from the hospital after yet another health crisis. But this time the doctors said there was nothing more they could do for him, and that it was just a matter of time.

We were saddened by this news, but accepted it. My family was more spiritual than religious, though we were Christian and definitely believed in God. My mother prayed a lot and believed in the hereafter, but she also loved anything supernatural. She often visited fortune tellers, spiritual advisors. and psychics, which my father accepted without comment. He would tease her by saying, "Cross my palm with five bucks and I'll tell you anything you want to know!" He believed in God, but was not the least bit religious, nor did he believe in such things as the afterlife or angels. He never prayed that I know of, and would always roll his eyes in a teasing sort of way when my mother would say grace at meals, a recitation that seemed to go on forever as she blessed everyone she could think of, including all servicemen, policemen, and firemen. Sometimes her blessings went on so long that our food got cold!

One night I was in my room asleep when, around 3 a.m., I heard my mother cry out for me. I rushed into my parents' bedroom to find my father sitting at the foot of their bed, sobbing. I hugged him and asked him what was wrong. He said that Nana (my grandmother, who died before I was born) had come into the room and asked him to go with her. He said that he wasn't ready and didn't want to go. He kept saying, "No, Nana, no! I don't want to go yet!"

I was shocked to hear this coming from my father because he had always been a nonbeliever in such things. He finally stopped crying, but refused to sleep in their bedroom again after that. We bought a hospital bed the next day, which we placed in the living room. We knew that my father's time was limited, so we did whatever he wanted. A few days after my father's bizarre Nana experience, we got a call that my Aunt Myrtle in Chicago had died unexpectedly. She and my dad were extremely close, although she was my mother's sister. We all decided not to tell my dad that Aunt Myrtle had died because it would be too hard on him, since he was now very ill. Two days later, as I performed my daily ritual of bringing him a little oatmeal, which he rarely finished, he turned to me and said, "Myrtle died." There was no way he could have known, so I said, "No, daddy, she's fine. Why would you say that?" He looked at me and said something I'll never forget: "Because she was just here."

My daddy died at home two days later, on June 11th. It was and always will be one of the saddest days of my life. When I think of my dad, I think of how much he loved his family and, yes, his wonderful sense of humor.

I continued to live at home with my mother even though I was getting restless and eager to get my own apartment. My mother was very protective of me and had never really explained the facts of life to me, so I was, shall we say, a late bloomer. Sex was never discussed in my house and even though my sister, Audrey, and I were really close, she was away so much of the time that we never really had the opportunity to talk about such things.

Needless to say, I was pretty innocent when I did start dating for real, as opposed to the fake dates I often went on for the fan magazines. One such encounter was with Dennis Wilson of the Beach Boys. He picked me up in his Jaguar XKE and we went to dinner. When we pulled up to my house afterwards, we kissed a little bit in his car, and then he tried to put my hand down his pants. I was shocked beyond belief! I slapped his face and got out of his car as quickly as I could. Not surpris-

A group of friends help me celebrate my 21st birthday. On the left is Cynthia Pepper and her husband, Buck; Tony Dow; me; Jimmy Hawkins, who starred in *Annie Oakley*; Peter Helm; and Brooke Bundy.

ingly, I never heard from Dennis again. A similar thing happened when I went out with Dean of the singing duo Jan and Dean. Everyone seemed to want what I wasn't ready to give up.

I lived at home until I was 23, at which time I finally decided I just had to get out on my own. My mother was not happy about my decision because I think she would have liked me to live with her forever. I found an apartment on Barham Boulevard, near the Warner Brothers studios, for $90 a month, and moved in. My mother refused to talk to me for several weeks and told me that I could take "absolutely nothing" with me, not even my own bedroom set or any of the furniture, all of which I had paid for. By then, acting jobs had really slowed down and I wasn't sure how I was going to make it because I had no savings and all of the money I had made had been spent keeping up the big white house in which we lived. However, I knew it was time to move on.

So I moved into my new apartment without my mother's blessing, which troubled me greatly because I don't like confrontation or discord of any kind. I guess you could say I'm a bit of a wuss, as I will do almost anything to avoid an argument. However, this was the one time I knew that I couldn't give in to my mother or she wouldn't let me leave home until I was 85! It was difficult, but I told her I was moving out with or without her permission. After all, I was 23, an adult, and I didn't really need her okay. We didn't speak for a few weeks, which was totally foreign to me because I had come from such a demonstrative and loving family. But I had to stand my ground, so there I was, living in an empty apartment with basically nothing.

One of my friends gave me a sofa with no legs that his parents were going to throw away, and the previous tenant had left an old redwood picnic table in the back yard, the kind with the two wheels on one end and a hole in the middle for an umbrella, which became my dining room table once I draped a tablecloth over it. I also had a coffee table made out of a long board and two stacks of bricks for support. And I had candles everywhere. In fact, my brother George came by one day and said my place looked like "the house of wax." But it was home to me and I was happy to feel so independent, though I didn't have a clue as to how I was going to support myself.

My mother finally called and, happily, we were able to patch things up. She even gave me a few dishes. But then she surprised me by saying she had sold our house and the buyer wanted it as is, which meant with all the furniture in it. Three years had passed since my dad had died and my mother was lonely, so she decided that she was going to move to Florida to marry my Uncle Herbie, who had been married to my Aunt Nettie, but was now a widower. My mother and Uncle Herbie had known each other since high school so they were comfortable together, though my mother said their marriage was just for companionship. I knew I would miss her, but I also knew I had to get on with my life, so I gave her my blessing. Uncle Herbie would never take my dad's place but he was a good man and I knew he would take wonderful care of my mom.

After the house sold, I met my mother for dinner, and then we went clothes shopping. She bought me a beautiful pantsuit and gave me $50 in cash—my payment from the sale of the house. I was dumbfounded because I had paid for that house, but my name was never put on the title. When Audrey found out, she broke down and cried because she had always been very protective of me, but there was nothing anyone could do. I was on my own, my mother was moving to Florida, and my life was in transition.

Despite the disappointment of not receiving anything from the sale of the house, I don't feel that my mother was a bad person. I know she loved me very much. I guess she just didn't think about what was right and had convinced herself that everything was fine. The few people who knew what happened asked me if I was angry or if I hated my mother for it ‾ I told them no, I could never hate my mother. I know she meant well and would never intentionally hurt me. What was done was done and I had to move on.

Living in my own apartment, I finally felt like an adult. I only had myself to answer to and no curfew. I was finally on my own and loving it, but still concerned as to how I was going to pay my bills. It was around that time that I was introduced to marijuana by the guys who lived across the street. Drugs were rampant back then and I have no idea how I was spared getting caught up in them like so many of my fellow performers did. My life had been very protected—no drugs, alcohol, or smoking— and now here I was getting stoned most every weekend with my neighbors. Luckily, that's about as rebellious as I ever got.

Because acting jobs were becoming fewer and fewer, I took a job as a receptionist at a private school to pay the bills. I had to wing it because I didn't have a clue as to what I was doing. Then I worked as a cocktail waitress at the Ice House in Pasadena. Again, I didn't have a clue as to what I was doing, but that job gave me new found respect for people in the service industry because waiting tables is incredibly hard work. From there I worked for a very short time at a fish-and-chips place in Burbank. That job ended when a drunk woman who thought her husband was eyeing me (he wasn't, as far as I could tell) grabbed me and beat the crap out of me. It took three men to pull her off, and I ended up with a lot of bruises and a black eye.

I tried many different jobs but was not very good at any of them because the only thing I really knew how to do was act. I finally took a job as a telephone operator at KHJ, a radio station in Hollywood. It was there that I met a DJ by the name of Humble Harv. He was quite popular in Los Angeles at the time and he desperately wanted me to go out with him. The only problem was that Harv was married. He told me how unhappy he was and how his wife was a horrible person. He said that he would have to smash his fists into the wall so as to prevent himself from killing her. I told him I wouldn't sleep with him, since he was married, but we could be friends. He wanted more, so our relationship consisted primarily of occasional phone chats. Several months after I left that job I saw Harv on the news—he had been arrested for murdering his wife! The episode gave me chills.

One day, I found myself down and out, and totally depressed. I hadn't had an acting job in a couple of years, I was doing odd jobs that I hated, and I felt like a total failure. I fell on my bed and cried, praying to God to give me a sign as to what to do. A few minutes later I got up to dry my tears and as I was walking to the bathroom my phone rang. It was a call to go on an audition for a show called *Getting Together*, starring Bobby Sherman. I was shocked because it literally came out of the blue.

It had been a long time since I'd been before a camera and I was feeling a little rusty. My worst fears came true when I got to the audition and saw lots of girls in the waiting room. I gave it my best shot but wasn't feeling confident the way I did when I had been working all the time. The next day I got a call from the casting agent to tell me that the role was between me and a wonderful actress named Brooke Bundy. I was sure she would get the part because she was far prettier than I was and had been working quite a bit ⁻ but much to my astonishment, I landed the role. When I found out, I almost fainted. It was a great part, and a wonderful experience. Bobby Sherman was a doll, and I now had enough money to pay my rent for the next several months. Life was good.

Shortly after that, I was called to work on a Jack Benny special at NBC. It was just a small part, but I got to work with Jack again and that was always special. We had stayed in touch but I never let on as to how broke I was. I'm sure he would have even given me money if I had asked, but I was too proud and too embarrassed.

So I went to work the next day in my little white Austin Healy Sprite. The guard at the front gate waved me onto the NBC lot, and just then, in the middle of a huge rainstorm, my car stalled. I tried and tried to get it started, but it just wouldn't turn over. Just then this adorable man got out of his car and started pushing me into a parking spot. He said he'd have someone call the auto club for me. We didn't have cell phones back then, but he assured me he'd have someone take care of it for me and then he left. I didn't even get his name and had no idea who he was, but I thanked him and ran to the stage so I wouldn't be late.

About an hour later, Irving Fein, Jack Benny's manager, said he wanted to introduce me to someone who had come from New York, a big honcho with the Benton and Bowles Advertising Agency. One of their clients was Texaco, and he was in Los Angeles because they were sponsoring the Jack Benny special. Irving said the agency did a lot of commercials and it wouldn't be a bad idea to meet him.

Well, you guessed it. In walked Merrill, the man who had pushed my broken-down car into a parking space. There was an immediate attraction and he asked me to dinner. We saw each other every night he was in Los Angeles and began a relationship that lasted for years. Merrill got me a job as a receptionist at Benton and Bowles, which I held for quite a long time, and it was there that I made many close friendships.

That was the good part. The bad part was that the man who had swept me off my feet was married, and had lied to me from the beginning. He was able to get away with it because he lived in New York and commuted to California every few weeks. After a few months, I was in love with him and envisioned being married to him. But one day, while we were having lunch at the Bel Air Hotel, Merrill told me that he couldn't continue the charade any longer because, he said, I was the sweetest person he knew and it was killing him to maintain the lie. When Merrill admitted all of this to me, it felt as if someone had kicked me in the stomach. I told him then that our relationship was over, but I was weak and continued to see him on and off for several years. Finally, I just couldn't live with the guilt and broke off our relationship once and for all, something I should have done much sooner.

When I decided to write this book, I struggled over whether to discuss the following incident, which occurred toward the end of my relationship with Merrill. However, after much thought and soul searching, I realized that it must be included if I was to be true to myself, as well as to you, the reader. I ask that you please not judge me too harshly as you read it, as no one should be judged until you've had the opportunity to walk in their shoes.

The incident was this: I found out that I was pregnant. Ordinarily this would have been wonderful news, but by then it was obvious that Merrill wasn't going to leave his family, and I was alone, broke, and struggling to make ends meet. What was I to do?

When I told Merrill, he went ballistic, saying that I needed to get an abortion immediately. At the time, that wasn't an option for me. Abortions were illegal then, so I told him that I was going to have the baby, even though I had no idea how I was going to take care of it. Merrill went crazy, saying that I would "ruin" him and his family if I went ahead with my plans, and that he would have absolutely no involvement other than to pay for an abortion. I was numb and almost comatose in my reaction. I had never felt so alone in my life, and I was too ashamed to tell anyone because I thought everyone would judge me and tell me what a horrible person I was. I couldn't even bring myself to tell my sister, Audrey, the person I was closest to. I know she wouldn't have judged me because she loved me unconditionally, but somehow, in my mind, I felt that I had let her down in some way, and I didn't want her to think less of me.

The only person I told was a very dear friend of mine, whose name I promised not to reveal. She was very concerned about me, so she arranged for me to meet a man who was a physician in Switzerland. He and his nurse/girlfriend flew to Los Angeles several times a year specifically to perform illegal abortions, often two or three a day, at $750 each, which was a lot of money back then.

I wasn't allowed to know the doctor's name, and payment had to be in cash. There were no cell phones back then, so all of the arrangements had to be done via payphone. It was incredibly sleazy, and it made me feel so cheap, but I had no other choice, so I agreed.

My friend did everything for me, and I don't know how I would have gotten through the experience without her. She picked me up and drove me to a specific phone booth, where the doctor told us where and what time to meet him. He worked out of an apartment building, and my friend was not allowed to come inside. She was told over the phone what time she could come pick me up.

I am now pro-choice because I believe a woman has the right to decide what is done to her body, but at the time I really wanted to have the baby, although I knew doing so would have made my life even more difficult. Merrill kept talking about being "ruined," yet I felt, through his insistence that I have an abortion, that I was the one being ruined.

I won't go into the procedure, other than to say it was a painful, horrible experience. Luckily, everything went well, and I was released at the given time with painkillers and instructions to stay in bed for a while. I was groggy, in pain, and felt that my life had hit rock bottom. As I exited the apartment building, I was greeted by my friend, her arms outstretched and a bouquet of flowers in her hand. She gave me a big hug and we both wept.

It was so difficult for me to seek forgiveness. For many years, I felt that God was punishing me for what I had done, and maybe that's why I was never able to have children. However, I know God is forgiving, so the hardest thing for me was forgiving myself. I've accepted my poor choice and have chosen to move forward. I'm not proud of that time in my life, but I can't change it. I'm so grateful that I have so many nieces and nephews to love, and my "children" are now my dogs and cats.

By the time I had left Merrill, my very good friend, Sharon Baird, had moved into the same apartment building that I lived in. We had met when we were about 10 or 11 and auditioned for the same role in *Professional Father*. A few years later, Sharon was working on the *Mickey Mouse Club* as one of the original Mouseketeers, and I was doing *Old Yeller* at the Disney Studio. We had school together every day in the big red trailer on the Disney lot, and during that time we became reacquainted and have been best friends ever since.

Sharon moved upstairs from me and we became inseparable. Almost every night we would have a hot fudge sundae with bananas and sit on our front steps and watch the world go by. One day, an apartment became available down the street. It had a fireplace, which I thought would be really fabulous to have, so I called to see if they could show it to me. The office agreed, so I dragged Sharon along with me. I fell in love with the apartment, but was crestfallen when I learned that the rent was $140 a month. Considering my financial situation, it might as well have been $1 million. I didn't want the manager to think I was wasting his time, so I did some quick thinking and said, "It's really nice but there's no room for my dining room table." At that point Sharon suddenly ran out, and I quickly followed. Sharon was laughing hysterically and had to get out before the manager of the complex saw her. I asked her what was so funny, and she said, "When you said there was no room for your dining room table, I wanted to say, 'Yeah especially when you put up the umbrella!'" She and I have laughed about that incident a million times over the years.

During my interesting "apartment days," my sister, Audrey, divorced her husband, Buzz, remarried, and moved to Spain. She had a son named Paul, who later legally changed his name to Niko. After ending the affair with my married paramour, I decided to get away and visit Audrey in Madrid. I didn't have much money but I scrimped and saved and sold a few things so I could go. I sublet my apartment to someone I barely knew but thought I could trust. He said he would pay my rent for me while I was gone, so I gave him the name and address of my landlord. My trusting nature got me in huge trouble because over the seven months that I was away this guy never paid a single cent of rent.

While I was still in Spain I got a frantic phone call from my mother. My landlord had her number in case of emergency and he told her that he didn't know what to do other than evict me for nonpayment of rent. I was thousands of miles away in Madrid, my mother was in Florida, and I was about to be cast into the street. Luckily, I was able to contact my landlord, who was a struggling actor himself and a really nice guy, and I explained my situation. While in Spain I got lucky and did a couple of commercials for Iberia Airlines, and asked him if he could give me two weeks so that I could return home and get things straightened out.

When I finally returned to my apartment, all I could think of was that it could have been worse. I didn't have much for my squatter to ransack, but the place was a mess. I found a few pair of panties and bras on my bedroom floor that were not mine, a hypodermic needle in the bathroom (also not mine) and, not surprisingly, the man I had trusted to take care of the place was no where to be found. The kicker is that he had actually sent me a few postcards while I was in Spain assuring me that everything was okay and that he had been paying the rent and taking care of the place for me. Of course, it was my own fault because I barely knew him, but he had seemed so nice and I was so happy that I had found someone to take care of my place while I was gone that I jumped at the chance. Luckily, my landlord understood that I had been duped, but I had to give him almost all of the money I had made in Spain to make up for seven months of back rent.

One night Sharon and I went to a club to go dancing and met two guys who were in the band playing that night. The guy that Sharon was attracted to was named Gene, and he was the lead singer and bass player. I was attracted to Rick, the trumpet player. Sharon dated Gene for several years and I ended up marrying Rick, who at that time was a struggling musician with little money. He had worked with Little Richard prior to the gig at which we met, but was fired when he refused Little Richard's sexual advances.

Rick moved in with me and we planned our wedding, which was a very low-key affair in Los Altos, where his parents lived. Though I cared for Rick very much, I quickly realized that getting married was a huge mistake. Rick was not ready to settle down and I eventually learned that he had several girlfriends the whole time we were married. The best thing that came out of that relationship was my friendship with his parents. I love them very much and they're still an important part of my life.

Rick and I had a lot of rough times during our years together, but there were good times too. Neither of us had any money so we were constantly struggling to make ends meet. I remember one weekend in which Rick's band was hired to perform at a local night club. When he came home, he opened his trumpet case to reveal that it was full of filet mignon, Porterhouse steaks, lobster tails, and other wonderful food. Rick had gone into the club's kitchen when no one was looking and stolen all the food from the freezer! I was appalled, as I had never stolen anything in my life, not even as a child when some of my friends would steal things like nail polish from the local dime store. I panicked for a moment because I knew he couldn't take the food back; but I also knew that we were dead broke and had no food in the house. So I prayed to God to please forgive Rick for stealing. The next day, Rick and I were driving somewhere and I asked him, "Honey what would you like for dinner tonight, the filet mignon or the lobster tail?" The absurdity of the whole thing made us laugh. We didn't have two cents to rub together and here I was asking him if he would prefer lobster tail!

After Rick and I got married we moved into a nicer apartment across from the Warner Brothers Studios, and later into a beautiful Spanish-style duplex. When Rick took a job as a mastering engineer on Stevie Wonder's best-selling album, *Innervisions*, money became less of an issue, so we decided to buy a little house in Burbank, complete with a real fireplace, hardwood floors, and a big backyard with lots of trees. We paid $36,000 for it, and I was thrilled because life finally started looking good. Rick, on the other hand, was not happy and soon asked for a divorce because a lot of cute girls were hanging around the recording studio and he wanted his freedom. We broke up and got back together again about five times, but it just wasn't meant to be. In the end, I got the house and he got his girlfriends, which he seemed to think was fair, as he didn't want any responsibility.

After Rick and I parted ways, I was having lunch with one of my best friends, Noni White, who later co-wrote the Disney movie *Newsies* (1992) with her wonderful husband Bob Tzudiker, when I was approached by a man named Richard Halsey, who said I looked familiar to him. He told me that they were casting a film titled *When the Line Goes Through* (1973), starring an unknown actor by the name of Martin Sheen and they were looking for an actress to play opposite him. They were considering Carol Lynley but were still auditioning, and Richard asked me if I would go and meet with the producer the next day. Richard hadn't asked for my phone number, and he appeared legitimate, so I figured what the heck. I hadn't worked in a very long time, so I got the necessary information and went to the production office the next day.

I read for Clyde Ware, the movie's producer/writer/director. Once again there were lots of girls waiting to read and I was fairly certain that I didn't have a chance. But Clyde seemed to like my reading and asked if I could come back the next day to meet the actor who would be starring in the film. At that time, Martin had done only one other film, also for Clyde Ware, a little flick which almost no one had seen. When I got there the next day and was called in to read with Martin, I was very impressed with his intensity and something told me that he had the makings of a star. I was only halfway into the reading when Martin turned to Clyde and said, "There's no need to have anyone else come in and read. She's the one." I was flattered at the compliment but had no clue about this production.

As it turned out, the movie was to be filmed in a little town in West Virginia called West Union, which was where Clyde was from. The town was so small that they didn't even have a motel, let alone a hotel, so they approached the town folk and offered to pay them for putting up the cast and crew. It was quite an experience. I played the twin of an actress named Davey Davison, who also happened to be Clyde's wife. Unfortunately, they were having marital problems at the time and for some reason Clyde was trying to make Davey jealous by constantly flirting with me. Davey assumed that Clyde and I had something going (we didn't), so our time together was rather awkward.

Nonetheless, I loved my role and I had my first screen kiss with Martin. However, the movie was less than great and as far as I know it was never released outside of West Virginia. After filming was completed, I received a call from Martin at home thanking me for doing such a fine job of acting. He agreed that the movie was a piece of crap, but he said that my scenes with him had made it all worthwhile. That call meant so much to me, as I thought he was an incredible actor. *When the Line Goes Through* was released on VHS. A friend of mine found it and mailed it to me with a sticker on the side that read: "Caution! Contents may cause drowsiness!"

Shortly after I returned home from filming, I was introduced to a cinematographer named John Goode. He moved in with me after my divorce from Rick, and then he bought a house and I moved in with him. We lived together for seven years. John was a wonderful man and I loved him very much; he had the best sense of humor of anyone I had ever met. The only drawback was that he was an alcoholic, and when he drank, he was horrible. I spent many nights at Al-Anon trying to understand his disease. It was only after we broke up that he finally got sober, and he later became a counselor for Alcoholics Anonymous. I'm happy to say that after our break-up we became very good friends. He later became a cameraman on *The Drew Carey Show* and became quite successful. Sadly, he died a few years ago from a heart attack, and even though we hadn't been together for many years, I took it very hard.

Our relationship was very volatile throughout. We twice set a date to get married, but John's drinking scared me because it made him so mean, unlike my brother, who became sweeter and funnier after he'd had a few. John would threaten to kill me when he was drunk, and completely forget about it the next day. This, I later learned, was because he was in a blackout. Despite all this, my family loved John and he loved them. (Of course, I never told them that he had threatened to kill me.)

During my relationship with John, my nephew, Howard, came for a brief stay. Howard was an incredibly talented hairdresser and eventually became the stylist for the rock group Chicago. He started making really good money and, sadly, spent a lot of it on drugs. Before too long, Howard was in pretty deep.

In an effort to get his life back together again, Howard asked if he could stay with John and me until he got things sorted out. One day I was supposed to pick John up at the airport, so Howard decided to tag along. I went in to take a shower and later, when I walked out into the backyard to tell Howard I was ready to go, I couldn't find him. I looked all over the house and finally found him at the bottom of our pool. I screamed, and then I blacked out. Almost instantly, it seemed, all of our neighbors were there, along with the police, the fire department, the coroner, paramedics, and my family. The first responders did what they could, but Howard was dead. That was one of the worst days of my life. It's been many years, but not a day goes by that I don't think of Howard and how things might have been different if I hadn't left him alone so I could take a shower. Howard and I were extremely close our whole lives. We talked on a daily basis and he always signed off after our conversations with "I love you, Bev." The day he died, I lost a piece of my heart.

Around this time there was an actors' strike in Hollywood, which also affected work for cinematographers like John. I still owned my little house and had it as a rental but John's house was about to go into foreclosure, so I took out a loan against my house to save his house. But I ended up losing my house and then we ended our relationship, so once again I was lost.

I found a little guest house for rent in North Hollywood and got ready to start over. My plan was to avoid men all together because I just seemed to be unlucky in love. I had an agent, Steve Stevens, but work eluded me, so I took a variety of odd jobs, including a receptionist position at a law firm. However, I really had to wing it because I had absolutely no clerical skills at all. I did make a lifelong friend there, however, so I guess it wasn't a total loss.

I kept my married name, Collins, because I felt that my acting career was over and that no one really cared. I was in "woe is me" mode and stayed there for quite some time. In the movie business there are several unions that you must belong to in order to work. For actors, the biggest is the Screen Actors Guild, or SAG. Members must pay their dues twice a year, and I continued to do so even during the dry years because I guess, deep down, I always believed that things would pick up. I also maintained my membership in the American Federation of Television and Radio Artists (AFTRA), which is required for work in taped or live shows such a soap operas, awards shows, and radio shows.

Back then there was another union, the Screen Extras Guild (SEG). I didn't belong to that one because I had never worked as an extra, but my brother, George, was a rep for the guild and had a lot of clout. He knew I was struggling and asked me if I would like to join; they didn't take everyone, but he said he could get me in if I was interested. I told my agent, Steve, that I was going to join SEG and he had a fit. He said he was trying to get me work, but would have even greater difficulty if I was working as an extra. I realized he was right, but I was starting to get desperate, and work as an extra was better than no work at all. I had rent due and pets (not to mention myself) to feed. Steve told me that if I had to do it to use my married name so no one would know, and to stay in the background so I wouldn't be recognized.

So I joined SEG, which has since merged with the Screen Actors Guild, and got my first job as an extra. I stayed in the background so as not to be noticed (although by now no one seemed to know who I was anyway) and it was a very weird feeling. I was used to having makeup, hair, and wardrobe done for me, as well as having my own dressing room. Now, I was literally just part of the crowd. Please don't get me wrong—there's nothing wrong with being an extra: It's an honest job and necessary to filmmaking, but few extras ever rise above that. It's almost a stigma: once an extra, always an extra. And extras aren't always treated with a lot of respect.

I wondered if this was now my destiny. Ironically, Steve called the next day to tell me that I had gotten a small part in the television series *Hotel*, starring James Brolin. It was just three lines, but I was thrilled. When I got to the set, I was rushed into hair, wardrobe, and make-up, and then shown to my dressing room. I was so grateful and happy to be there. But while I was sitting in the makeup chair, the makeup man turned to me and said, "Honey, if you want a doughnut, you'd better go get one now before those fucking extras eat them all!" I sat there dumbfounded, unable to believe what I had just heard. I had worked as an extra just two days before, but now, because I had three lines and a dressing room, that supposedly made me better than them. I knew that wasn't true.

Ever since, I've had great respect for people who work as extras. Sure, there are those who give the job a bad name by being late or lazy or stealing from the craft service table, but there are just as many who are extremely professional, show up on time, work hard, and try to make an honest living. Extras are an important part of every film because without them, a movie wouldn't be realistic. At that moment, while sitting in the makeup chair, I decided that I would always treat extras—and anyone I encountered while working—with even more kindness and respect than I did before. Thankfully, a lot of big names feel the same way. Michael Landon, for example, was famous for being kind and friendly to extras, as is Martin Sheen and Angela Lansbury. In fact, Angela showed tremendous regard for the extras on *Murder, She Wrote*. Toward the beginning of the series, I was told, she walked onto the set and saw two tables: one piled high with goodies for the cast and crew, and one with just donuts for the extras. Angela turned to the person in charge of crafts services and said, "I'm going back to my dressing room, and when I come back, I want that second table to look exactly like the first!" Talk about a classy lady.

Extras today are treated a little better than they were back in my day. I've started hearing assistant directors refer to them as "background artists," which I like a lot. I was talking to a "background artist" one day and he told me that he had recently worked with Martin Sheen on a film. On one blistering hot day, he said, he and several other guys were in Army fatigues standing on a hill waiting to shoot a scene when they looked over and saw Martin Sheen climbing up the hill carrying as many bottles of water as he could hold—for the extras! The man said he will tell that story for the rest of his life because they were all so touched by Martin's kindness.

To backtrack a little: I mentioned earlier that my sister, Audrey, was married to a stuntman by the name of Buzz Henry. He was quite well-known in the business and was close friends with Mike Connors, Glenn Ford, and Robert Fuller. He bought Audrey a diamond ring the size of a Buick and a beautiful home in Toluca Lake, but theirs was a "can't live with him, can't live without him" kind of relationship. They finally divorced and both re-married; my sister had a son and Buzz had a daughter. Buzz stayed in touch with our family even after the divorce because we were all very close. When I went to Madrid to mend my broken heart over my affair with "Married Merrill," Audrey and I had a long talk. She said, "You know, Weencie (her nickname for me), I love Alfonso (her new husband); he's a good man, a good husband, and a good father. But somehow there will always be Buzz in my life and I have a feeling that one day we will be together again."

Shortly after I returned from Spain, Buzz called to invite me to lunch. As we talked, he said to me, "You know, I love Pat, she's a wonderful woman, a good wife, and a good mother. But I can't get Audrey out of my system, and I think one day we'll be together again." It was eerie because it was almost the exact same conversation, verbatim, that I'd had with Audrey just a few months earlier. Buzz then said to me, "You know, I've always thought you were a good actress and you should be working again. I now have my own office at Paramount and I'm in a position to help you. I want you to call me on Thursday and I'll schedule a meeting for you to meet Mike Connors. I'm pretty sure I can get you a little part on *Mannix*."

Sadly, that meeting never took place because Buzz was killed that afternoon in a head-on collision. Ironically, his funeral was on Thursday, the day I was supposed to call him. Life can really throw some curves and it makes you realize how fragile we all are.

After taking a hiatus from men following my break with John, I started dating a guy named Richard, and quickly found myself falling in love with him. He was a terrific guy but he wanted to get married and have six kids. I was older than he was and I knew that such a plan wasn't realistic. So Richard met someone else and decided to marry her. Again, my heart was broken and I started thinking that it just wasn't in the cards for me to "live happily ever after" with my Prince Charming. Interestingly, Richard and I became reacquainted just a few years ago and have established a deep friendship. You never know what life has in store.

After Richard, I felt I was definitely done with men. I thought, too, that it just wasn't meant for me to ever act again. I continued working here and there as an extra under the name of Beverly Collins, and also worked as an office temp. I was sad, broke, unhappy, lost and wondering just what had happened to my life.

One day I was in Hollywood and stopped at a bookstore before I was supposed to be at one of my temporary office jobs. I looked up and there was Marvin Paige, a casting director with whom I had worked many times when I was younger. We talked briefly and I told him I was on my way to work. He asked me what show I was working on and I sheepishly told him that I was working as a receptionist. He told me I should be acting and to call him because he was the casting director for *General Hospital.* I called, and so began a lengthy stint on one of television's most popular soap operas.

I worked quite often, thanks to Marvin. Not always on camera, however. Sometimes I would be the voice on the paging system calling one of the doctors to the emergency room, or I would be at the nurses' station with a couple of lines. Nevertheless, I was thrilled, and extremely grateful to Marvin because he kept me busy on that show, which provided a financial buffer. Things were starting to come together, at least work-wise. I never had a big part on *General Hospital,* but I was treated very well, always had a dressing room, was allowed to drive on the lot and, as strange as it sounds, I even got some fan mail.

One night I went out to dinner with a friend I had met at the law firm where I had previously worked. Afterward, we went into the bar to have a drink and listen to the band. There was a group of guys there and one of them asked me if I wanted to dance. He had sparkling eyes and the greatest smile, so I said yes. It was the smartest thing I ever did because that man with the sparkling eyes became the love of my life, my second husband, Mike.

Mike and I talked and I was immediately attracted to him. He seemed quite interested in me as well. He bought me a drink and said that he and some of his co-workers were there with a group of people from American Express. Mike was assistant vice president of operations for Hilton Inns, which was part of Hilton Hotels. The first thing I asked him was if he was married because I certainly didn't want to go down that road again, and he told me he was divorced. Then I asked him if he had any children, and he said yes, two. I asked him their names and he said Buttons and Zippers. I looked at him quizzically as I thought those were two of the strangest names ever for children, and that's when he laughed and told me that his "children" were the canine kind. Wow! A man after my own heart! I love animals. They're my passion, perhaps because they love us unconditionally and, unlike people, they don't judge us. My good friend Celeste Yarnell, another actress and animal lover, has a bumper sticker on her car that reads: "A dog is the only being in the universe that loves you more than he loves himself." I love cats, too. In fact, I currently have three cats and three dogs. Because I love animals so much, it should come as no surprise that working on *Old Yeller* was a dream come true for me.

Mike won my heart with that statement and we exchanged phone numbers. By the time I got back home there was already a message from him. The next day, while sitting at home, I looked down my driveway to see a delivery person making his way to my door carrying the biggest balloon bouquet I had ever seen in my life. There were even paw prints on the balloons with a note that read, "Our dad would like to know if

Me and Mike at a Christmas party.

you'd have lunch with him. Love, Buttons and Zippers." I melted, and that was the beginning of our relationship.

Mike picked me up the next day and I loved how he treated my two dogs at the time, Barney and Daisy. That was always incredibly important to me, the way a man responded to my pets, because they were my "children" as well. For the most part, that was my deciding factor as to whether I would go out with someone on a second date. If they treated my dogs kindly, then yes. Otherwise, it was bye-bye!

Mike passed that test with flying colors, but I couldn't help but wonder if he, too, would somehow end up breaking my heart. However, we clicked immediately and never looked back. Before long we were inseparable and I couldn't believe how blessed I was to find such a wonderful man. A month after our first date Mike proposed, and although I never thought I'd marry again, I didn't hesitate to say yes. He was everything and more than I had ever wanted in a man.

Mike and I planned to get married a year to the day we met, April 11th. He, along with Buttons and Zippers, moved in with me in my little guest house, and we quickly settled into being a blended family. Everyone got along famously and things were good. I continued to work often on *General Hospital* and Mike at The Hilton in Beverly Hills. My guest house was small, so we decided to rent a larger house until we got married and figured out exactly where we wanted to live. We rented a nice house from my good friend Dennis Freeman, an actor friend who was looking for someone to rent his home.

By this time, my Uncle Herbie had passed away, and mother had returned to Los Angeles. She had an apartment for a while but was starting to develop Alzheimer's disease and could no longer live on her own, so we placed her in a retirement home, then into a convalescent home when her conditioned worsened.

My mother always used to say to me, "If I just knew you were married and taken care of, then I could die in peace." Sadly, by the time I had met Mike, she was so afflicted with dementia that she no longer recognized me. She got to meet Mike, but her condition was so far advanced that she had no idea who he was. That always made me sad because I know she would have loved him, and be happy knowing that I was no longer alone. That period was a very sad time for my family. My father had died, my nephew had died, my sister Dorothy had died, and now my mom had passed away.

When Mike and I got married, Audrey flew in from Hawaii, where she was living, to be my matron of honor. The ceremony was beautiful, but I was tinged with sadness because so many members of my family could not be there. Beyond that, however, my future had never looked brighter. I loved Mike and he loved me, and we were gloriously happy together.

Not long after we had gotten married, Mike called me while I was out shopping with my friend, Sharon. I had just gotten a cell phone, which were relatively new at the time and about the size of a quart of milk! When it rang, I jumped about three feet. Mike called to tell me that he was being transferred to Dallas, Texas, to help open up Hilton Suites. He asked if he had my support on this because he really wanted this job opportunity. Sharon and I were in the crystal department at one of my favorite stores, and when he told me the news I almost dropped the Waterford glass that I was holding. I turned to Sharon and, without skipping a beat, said, "We're moving to Texas!"

Mike was very excited about going to Texas because he saw it as a great career move. As for me, I was working here and there, but it wasn't like I was starring in a series. My role on *General Hospital* was something I was grateful for, but there were many times that I wasn't even on camera, just a voice on the paging system. So although I enjoyed being there, I felt that I couldn't stand in the way of Mike's career.

We made our plans and flew to Dallas to look at houses. I had never been to Dallas before, so it was quite an adventure. I was leaving many friends in Los Angeles, but I wasn't too concerned because I knew that friends are friends wherever you are, almost like angels—you don't have to see them to know that they are there. This has held true my whole life as I have good friends in California, Nevada, Texas, Florida, Connecticut, Ohio, Oregon, and Missouri, among other places.

Mike and I bought a beautiful home in Highland Shores, a suburb of Dallas. It came complete with a marble fireplace, sunken dining room, swimming pool, and Jacuzzi. We made quite a few friends, many of whom I'm still friends with today. Although acting was in my blood, I was content for the first time to just enjoy my "normal" life. I joined a bowling league, played bunco and pokeno, and did various crafts with my friends. Mike was recruited to be Santa Claus and the Easter Bunny for all of the kids in the neighborhood.

Then all hell broke loose. Within a very short period our little dog, Daisy, died; our cat, Evelyn, died; our cat, Weencie, died; and then we got the devastating news that Mike's father, George, had passed away. He was a wonderful man who I called Dad from the beginning.

We flew to Phoenix for the funeral and returned to the news that Hilton Suites was having problems and Mike's position had been eliminated. He no longer had a job, and I hadn't been working, so we were a little concerned. But Mike was always a positive person and confident that he would find another job quickly, though the kind of work he did was not something for which you just walked in and filled out an application.

Time started running out for us. With no work forthcoming, we quickly burned through all of our savings. We started to get behind in our payments, and that's when we started to panic. We finally reached the point where we had no savings at all, and we knew something had to be done fast.

A friend told us that they were hiring at Sonic, a popular hamburger joint. We had no choice but to consider it because Mike simply could not find a job, and I really had no skills other than acting. I fell into such a funk that I could barely talk. It all seemed so surreal to me; here we were, a former corporate executive and an actress who had literally made a fortune during her career, and now we were reduced to being carhops for $3.50 an hour plus tips.

In retrospect, it's a wonder our marriage survived. I was so depressed that all I did was cry. I never blamed Mike because it wasn't his fault, but I just couldn't figure out how we were going to get out of the mess we were in. My anxiety grew worse by the day.

One day at work, I waited on a couple of women. As I brought them their order, one of them said that I looked like an actress they remembered. "We can't remember her name," the woman said. "It 's Barbara or Beverly or something. We're not sure if you know who we're talking about, but she was a child actress who did a lot of work and she was a really good actress, but we haven't seen her in a long time. We know you're not her, of course, but we were just saying, wouldn't it be funny if this is where washed-up actresses end up." I didn't speak because I knew that if I tried, I'd just start crying. I smiled weakly and just walked away, wishing more than anything that the world would just swallow me up. Mike and I worked at Sonic for a few months and barely made enough money to put food on our table.

We finally sold our house, but by the time we paid everything off, including the overdue mortgage payments, the bank handed us a check for a paltry $500! We couldn't believe it. Now we had no money, no job, and no place to live. We looked at each other in disbelief, and then started crying. Our wonderful fairytale life had come to a screeching halt, and we had no idea what to do next.

I had read once that God sends us angels in different forms. I truly believe that because just when Mike and I were at our lowest, my wonderful friend, Sharon Baird, invited us to stay with her in Reno, Nevada until we were able to get back on our feet. She really was our angel in disguise because I'm not sure where we would have gone or what we would have done.

A group of friends in Dallas surprised us with a going-away party. They each gave us a card and told us not to open them until we got home. They explained that they couldn't decide what to buy for us so they decided to give us money instead. They asked us to accept it with love because that's the way in which it was given. Each card had money in it, some $10, some $20, and some $100. As we opened each card, Mike and I just wept, only this time they were tears of joy at the realization of what wonderful, kind, and caring friends we had. Even though we had next to nothing and no idea what the future held, we still felt like the two luckiest people in the world. It's something I'll never forget.

My niece, Jannine, flew in from Oregon to help us pack and ride with me to Reno because I would be driving one of our cars while Mike drove a U-Haul with all of the belongings and our second car hitched to it. With the $500 we got from the sale of our house, plus the money from our friends and the tips we had saved, we had a little over $2,000. We rented the U-Haul, packed up our belongings, and got ready to head west for our new adventure. As we prepared to pull out, our wonderful neighbors gave us a basket of sandwiches to eat along the way. As we drove off that fateful June morning, with all of our neighbors waving, I couldn't hold back the tears. What, I wondered, did God have in store for us?

It took us four days to drive from Dallas to Reno because Mike had to drive more slowly than usual due to the car he was towing behind the U-Haul. Our dog, Stanley, kept him company, and Jannine and I had the two cats, plus Barney, Buttons and Zippers, along with litter boxes, cat carriers, dog and cat beds, food, and water. Unloading and reloading the car each time we stopped was an ordeal in itself. Three of the nights, we got stuck with a room on the second floor, so trying to sneak in all of our stuff plus six animals was no easy feat! Our little dog, Barney, was getting really old and would sometimes bark for no reason, so at the recommendation of our veterinarian we gave him tranquilizers so he wouldn't give us away.

Me and my dear husband, Mike, shortly before he died of cancer.
His passing left a huge hole in my heart.

The first night, Mike and I wanted to take all of the dogs out so they could go potty. As I went to pick up Barney, he was as limp as a rag. I started screaming, "Oh my God, I've killed Barney!" This couldn't be happening, I thought. What were we supposed to do with a dead dog in the middle of nowhere? We couldn't just leave him there, but we also couldn't take him on the road with us for three more days. Then Jannine turned to me and said, "I think he's still breathing." I couldn't sleep at all that night, and prayed and prayed that little Barney would come out of it.

In the morning, he was still limp and not moving, but he was still breathing, so we wrapped him in a blanket and put him in the car. As I was driving (and praying), Jannine kept checking on him, but he still wasn't moving. I kept asking her if he was breathing, and she assured me that he was. Barney stayed that way, unmoving, for several hours, and then Jannine shouted, "He lifted his head!" My prayers had been answered. Understandably, that was the last time I gave Barney a tranquilizer.

Thankfully, the rest of the trip was pretty uneventful. But by the time we paid for the U-Haul, gas, motels, food, and the storage place for our belongings when we arrived, we had just $67 to our name.

Sharon welcomed us with open arms and a huge heart. How blessed we were to have such a kind, loving, and generous friend! In addition to seeing Sharon, I was also looking forward to seeing my brother, George, and his wife, Linda, who were living in Los Angeles. We talked every day, and George said he couldn't wait to see us. Their plan was to drive to Reno from Los Angeles and meet us on July 12. I couldn't wait. But on July 1, as we were barbequing in the back yard, the phone rang. It was George's best friend calling to tell me that George had suffered a heart attack and died. I screamed and dropped to my knees. It was as though my heart had been ripped out. Mike and Sharon came running in to comfort me. I don't remember the rest of the day. We didn't have enough money to fly to Los Angeles for George's funeral, so Mike borrowed the money from his mother. I was determined to attend my brother's funeral, even if we had to hitchhike.

Once we were settled in, Mike and I both took jobs at Macy's. Mike sold men's suits and I sold ladies' handbags. I was happy to have a job, but I felt like a robot going to work each day. It was boring work and I was miserable.

We stayed with Sharon for three months, and I still don't know how she managed to put up with us in addition to our six animals. Two months after we arrived, we had to put our little Barney down. He wouldn't eat or drink, he would just walk in circles and wet himself as a result of his "doggie dementia." It was just another tragedy for me to face, and I kept wondering when all the sadness in my life was going to end.

Mike and I finally managed to save enough money to get our own place. We rented a little town home not far from Sharon and continued to work at Macy's. I missed being an actress, but felt that I had to put that dream behind me and do my best as a sales associate, another job for which I had no experience. Audrey came to visit us and we cried together because she had always been my biggest fan and supporter. She told me not to give up on my dream of acting again because God wouldn't have given me the talent just to have it taken away from me. Having her there touched my heart. Little did I know that that would be the last time I would see her.

We stayed in Reno for a year and a half, then a friend of Mike's named Howard Wilkonson, called and offered him a job in Los Angeles. We jumped at the opportunity, though we knew we would miss Sharon terribly. We gave our notice at Macy's and off we went to L.A.—again not knowing what the future would hold.

Mike and I found a cute little house to rent in Woodland Hills, and I began a wonderful friendship with Howard's wife, Pam, in addition to making new friends and getting back together with old ones. One day Mike and I were on the way to the market when I said, "Honey, stop the car! I think that's Tony Dow walking to his car!" I hadn't seen Tony in years. I yelled, "Tony, it's me, Beverly!" We talked and hugged, and I told him that we had just moved back to Los Angeles. He immediately invited us to dinner, where I got to meet his wife, Lauren, who is one of the sweetest people in the world. Thus began our reunited friendship.

My nieces, Linnea and Jannine, and Linnea's husband, Elmo, were also living in Los Angeles, taking care of their mother (my sister-in-law), Anne. The day that Mike and I moved into our new house, I received the news that Anne had passed away. We all miss her to this day. But other than that sadness, life finally seemed to be turning around for us. Then my cat, Dennis, who was 18 and like a son to us (something only animal lovers will be able to relate to) became ill and I had to have him put down. I held him in my arms as he slipped away, and I thought I'd never stop crying. Shortly after that, Buttons developed liver failure and we had to have her put down too. What was happening? Just as things were finally starting to get good for us, sadness had found us once again.

Audrey had moved to Virginia with her husband, Lee. She told me that she hadn't been feeling well, but didn't let on that she had cancer. I talked to her almost every day, and though she sounded weak and tired, she managed to hide the fact that she was gravely ill. One evening when I called, Lee told me that Audrey was sleeping and that she was complaining of being cold. I still didn't have much money, so my niece, Georgia, and I went to a thrift shop and bought as many warm sweaters as we could, and mailed them, along with my winter coat, to her.

Sadly, Audrey never got to wear them. Three days after I mailed the package I received a call from Lee that she was dying. I called Mike at work, crying hysterically, and told him that I needed to be there with her. He rushed home and booked a flight out for 7 p.m. that evening. I couldn't think straight, so Georgia came into my bedroom and packed for me because I was in a daze.

Then the phone rang again. Mike answered it, and a moment later came into the bedroom, tears streaming down his face. "I'm sorry, honey," he said. "She's gone." All I remember of that moment is screaming, "No! No! No!" Audrey died on November 10, two weeks before my 50th birthday.

The year before she died, Audrey had sent me two beautiful angels made out of a very delicate material, like bisque or porcelain. One angel is lying down and blowing a kiss to the other. In the accompanying card, Audrey said that the angels represented the two of us and the one blowing the kiss was her. She said that she had the same pair and that every time she saw them on her coffee table, she was reminded of me.

The February after Audrey's death, we experienced a huge earthquake. The bricks tore from our house and were laying in the street, our fireplace pulled away from the wall, and we could see the outdoors. Every dish, glass, and plate that we had was thrown from the cupboards and shattered on the floor. There was so much broken glass everywhere that we could barely walk around. The destruction was massive.

And then something surreal happened, something I wouldn't have believed if I hadn't seen it with my own eyes. Sitting amongst all the rubble and debris were the two delicate angels that Audrey had given me—in perfect condition! My heart started pounding as I picked them up. How could they be the only things to survive unbroken when so much had been destroyed? All I can think is that there MUST be angels! I was so happy to still have that very special final gift from my beloved sister—something I will have until I die.

As I came to grips with my grief, I realized that my desire to act had never gone away. In fact, I wanted to act more now than I ever had before. But it had been so long since I'd performed in front of a camera, and no opportunities seemed available to me. Then one day, out of the blue, I got a call from Kevin Corcoran, the actor who had played little Arliss Coates in *Old Yeller*. I hadn't seen him in years, yet somehow he had tracked me down. He told me he was now an assistant director on *Murder, She Wrote* and offered me a small role. It was just two lines, but I would be acting again! I was so thrilled that you would have thought they were putting my footprints in Grauman's Chinese Theatre!

Shortly after that, I got a call from my friend Paul Petersen, who had co-starred in *The Donna Reed Show*. He told me that there was an autograph show in Hollywood put on by Ray and Sharon Courts called The Hollywood Collector Show, in which celebrities visit with fans and sell autographed pictures. I was amused, and wondered, who would want to buy an autographed picture of me? The whole concept seemed so strange because I was from an era in which movie stars willingly gave away autographs for free. I decided to give the show a try, and to my amazement, everyone was so generous and warm. They bought photo after photo, and I was just flabbergasted at the response.

I ran into Cynthia Pepper at the show, and I thought she was a guest like me. After all, she had played opposite Elvis Presley in *Kissin' Cousins*, appeared in *My Three Sons*, and even had her own series, *Margie*. It turned out, however, that Cynthia had come as a spectator and dropped by my table. We quickly became reacquainted and have since become lifelong friends. I suggested that she should do the show, too. It was a great experience because I was among friends and peers, and I ran into colleagues I hadn't seen in ages, such as Steve Stevens (who is now my agent) and Jon Provost of *Lassie* fame. (His wife, Laurie, now books me into various shows.) I suddenly felt like I was back in my element.

Then something strange and wonderful happened. Jack Hill, the director of *Spider Baby*, called to tell me that the film was finally going to be released, and that there was going to be a special midnight screening at the Nuart Theater in Los Angeles. Midnight, I thought…that's way past my bedtime, and who would go to a screening at midnight? We had filmed *Spider Baby* many years before, but legal problems prevented it from being released. However, Jack, Sid Haig, and Johnny Legend managed to finally overcome those issues, so the film could finally get a proper viewing. I was excited by the news, but still wondered who would go out at midnight for a little-known horror film.

I attended the midnight showing with Mike, Georgia, and her then-boyfriend, Joe, who is now her husband. We couldn't believe the scene! There was a line of people waiting to enter the theater that must have wrapped around the block. I was in shock. This was all so amazing to me. The response to *Spider Baby* was and remains overwhelming.

Aside from still feeling emotionally drained over Audrey's death, things actually seemed like they were looking up for us. *Spider Baby* enjoyed a resurgence and I started getting calls from reporters from various magazines eager to interview me. I also started getting fan mail again, as well as more and more calls to appear at autograph shows. I was finally doing again what I really loved when, without warning, the company that Mike worked for folded and he was again out of work.

Howard Wilkonson helped Mike find another job, but it required him to drive 90 minutes each way every day. Mike loved the people at the company, PCSC, and made some nice friends, some of which I'm still in touch with today, but he always believed he had made a mistake by leaving Hilton Inns and moving over to Hilton Suites, which never took off. He felt like a failure, but always tried to remain optimistic. Yet, despite the smile that always seemed to grace his face, I knew deep down that he was very unhappy.

One day we got a call from our friend, Dennis Freeman. He was planning on buying a big house in Las Vegas, and wanted us to live in it until he retired. The rent was minimal, and it would put us in a big, two-story house complete with pool, Jacuzzi, three fireplaces, and formal dining room. It was an incredible offer. Dennis didn't want to rent to strangers and knew we would take good care of it until he retired in seven years. What were we to do? Luckily, PCSC told Mike that he could do his job from Vegas because he typically made his sales by phone anyway, so the answer seemed obvious. Once again we packed our things and set off to live in Las Vegas.

Until then, my feeling about Las Vegas had been that it's a nice place to visit, but why would you want to live there? However, I knew that Mike wanted a fresh start, and he was very excited about the move. I had mixed emotions because I wanted him to be happy and I knew that he felt unfulfilled in Los Angeles, but I also didn't want to put my career on hold again. Mike left the decision up to me, which was typical of him. He always wanted me to be happy.

I ultimately decided that we should make the move, though deep down I feared that I would never work again. My niece, Linnea, drove to Las Vegas with us to help us get settled. It felt like deja vu, driving off into the unknown, me and Linnea in one car with the dogs and cats while Mike drove the U-Haul behind us.

(Here's a funny story: Shortly after moving to Las Vegas, I went shopping for a new pair of pants at a local store. I needed a size 8, but for some reason the rack seemed to be filled with a lot of size 2s, a few 6s and a size 10 – but no size 8. I was about to give up when I was approached by a sales lady who couldn't have been more than four feet tall. In fact, she was so short that she made ME look tall! And when she spoke, she sounded exactly like James Earl Jones! She asked me if she could help me find my size, then proceeded to flip through the rack saying, "Here's a deuce...another deuce...a six...a ten and another deuce." It was so comical to me that she kept saying "deuce" for the pants that were a size 2. All I could think was, "This woman has been in Vegas a little too long!"

Mike and I moved to Las Vegas in 1995, and made many new friends. I currently live in nearby Green Valley, in a retirement community jokingly known among the residents as Viagra Falls! I've grown to love the area, though it feels a little empty without Mike at my side, and I guess I'll be here until I have a good reason to move elsewhere, or God points me in another direction.)

It turned out that my career fears were unfounded. I landed an agent right away and got the first part I tried out for, a commercial for a Las Vegas furniture store. Then I auditioned for a commercial for a local casino, and got that one too.

Suddenly I was on a roll. Next up was an audition to be Beverly D'Angelo's stand-in for National Lampoons' *Vegas Vacation* (1997), starring Beverly, Chevy Chase, and Randy Quaid. If I got hired, I would work steadily for three months. I was excited because I thought it would be so much fun to be on a set with Chevy Chase!

I landed the job, and Beverly was wonderful, so kind and thoughtful. Chevy Chase, on the other hand, was not. In fact, even though I saw him every day, he would not even say hello to me. It saddened me to find out what an unpleasant, unkind person he really was. Whenever I said hello to him, he simply looked away, as if I didn't exist. I didn't expect him to carry on a conversation with me or even ask me how my day was, but really, how hard is it to smile? Sadly, he was like that to everyone who was not on his level.

Here's a little secret: Chevy and Beverly had great chemistry on screen, but off screen they couldn't stand each other. We went to Los Angeles for the last three days of shooting and on the final day, as Chevy was driving away, I saw Beverly run up to the car. I thought she was going up to him to say goodbye, but as she got close to the car she just stopped and flipped him the finger! That was how they ended their last day of shooting! Wow…the Griswolds…*who knew?*

After Mike and I settled in Las Vegas, I started to land a lot of local commercials, and received numerous invitations to attend autograph shows around the country. I also was contacted by a company called Slanted Fedora, which wanted me to attend regional *Star Trek* conventions. It was billed as the Fab Four tour and consisted of Jimmy Doohan (Scotty), George Takei (Sulu) Walter Koenig (Chekov), Nichelle Nichols (Uhura), and me. They were the Fab Four and I was the added guest.

The tour was great fun and I loved every minute of it. Even though I was only in one episode, "The Deadly Years," in which I played Lt.

Arlene Galway, the fans were so warm and receptive to me. In fact, being on that tour was one of the highlights of my career. The five of us got along famously and had the best time.

By then, I had gotten the bug and wanted to do more. I started attending more and more autograph shows, and loved every minute of it. The fans who greeted me were wonderful, and I had many funny and touching experiences.

For example, one time I was sitting next to Tommy Kirk, who played Travis in *Old Yeller*. We were sitting side by side with the stills from the movie in front of us when a woman walked up to us. She looked at Tommy, then looked at me, then looked at our photos, then looked at us again and finally said, "I can't believe I'm meeting you! *Old Yeller* was one of my favorite movies. I must have seen it 20 times and it's so amazing to me that you're both still alive!" Tommy and I didn't know what to say, so we didn't say anything. We just sat there and smiled.

At another show, a man walked up to my table and said, "When I read that you were going to be here, I was trying to place you. I couldn't put the name with the face, but now that I'm here, and I see all your pics, I know exactly who you are…you were that little girl who was always crying and whining!"

Then there was the man who hung around my table for about 20 minutes and didn't have a clue as to who I was. I asked him if he had seen *Old Yeller*. He shook his head no. I asked him if he had seen *The Lone Ranger*. He shook his head no. How about *Superman and the Mole Men*? Again, he shook his head no. *Star Trek*? Nope. I then asked him if anything on my table looked familiar and he again shook his head. I sat there in silence for a couple of minutes, not knowing what to say because he never spoke a word to me—all he did was shake his head no when I asked him if anything looked familiar. Then, as if a light bulb had gone on over his head, he looked at me and said, "Oh my gosh, I finally know who you are! I remember you now—you were Dorothy in *The Wizard of Oz*!" Unfortunately, he was serious. I didn't have the heart to tell him that it was Judy Garland who played Dorothy, and she was dead!

Then there was the guy who stood at my table and talked to me for about 45 minutes, looking at photos and remembering just about everything. He kept saying, "I remember HER in this" and "I remember HER in that. SHE was the little girl who did this…" Then he turned to me and asked, "So what is SHE doing now?" That's when I realized that he thought I was a vendor selling

Beverly Washburn photos, so I said, "That's me!" He looked at me incredu-
lously and said, "Get out of town!" It was hilarious: all that time and he didn't
know it was me. He kept talking about Beverly in the third person!

At another show, I had a fan who couldn't make up his mind about
which photo to buy. He kept going back and forth, stating how each one
was his favorite. He finally settled on two of them. I asked his name
(Robert), and signed them for him. He took them and then said, "Are
you in any of these?" I was stunned. He had purchased two photos from
me and didn't even know they were of me!

One time at the Hollywood Collectors Show, a very nice man approached my table, looked at all of my photos and said, "Wow, look at
you! You've been in everything. What an impressive body of work. When
did you get started, in the '30s?" Whoa! I wasn't even born until 1943! I
said to him, "I'd better get out the Oil of Olay. I must look worse than I
thought!" He apologized and we both had a good chuckle.

I've never been one to simply sign my name, unless specifically
asked to do so. I usually write, "Love, Beverly Washburn," or "Best wishes,"
or "Love and blessings." One year I was a guest at a very busy show and I
guess I was hurrying a little too much. I signed a photo for a fan, who
looked it over for a moment with a baffled expression and said, "Excuse
me, but I think you just wrote "Best Washes, Beverly Wishburn!"

More recently, I was at a festival in which someone asked for a
photo from *Star Trek*. The picture she wanted was one in which I'm
standing next to William Shatner and the rest of the crew. There's not a
lot of room to write on that particular photo, so by the time I wrote
across myself, my signature ended up across Captain Kirk's crotch! (Sorry,
Captain!) When I realized what I had done, I laughed and apologized,
and told the fan I would give her another one. By this time she was
laughing, too, and said that she preferred the first one.

My favorite fan incident, however, occurred when an adorable young
guy came up to my table to buy a *Star Trek* photo. A lot of celebrities
have a banner over their table containing their name and maybe the
name of the show they're best remembered for. I didn't have a banner, so
the guy asked me if I would be there the next day, as he worked at a
banner shop. I said yes, I would be there the next day, and he hurried off.
The next day he came up to my table with a huge banner that he had
made for me. He taped it up behind my table and said it was a gift from
him to me. I was so touched—until I actually read it. Instead of reading

"Beverly Washburn—America's Sweetheart," it said, "Beverly Washburn—America's <u>Swea</u>theart!" I didn't want to hurt his feelings by telling him about the misspelling, so I spent the remainder of the show billed as "America's Sweatheart!"

To this day, I'm not sure why people want to buy photos of me, but I'm extremely grateful that they do. The occasional oddball aside, movie fans tend to be gracious and friendly. Another reason I like to do autograph shows is that they give me the opportunity to give back, as I always donate a portion of the money I make to my favorite animal charities. And just so you know, dear reader, I will also donate a portion of the profits from this book to an animal charity because animals are my passion.

Invariably, there will be someone at an autograph show who says something that touches my heart and makes me cry. They're the people who say that they watched me growing up, or that they followed my career, or that I touched their lives in some special way. One man told me that meeting me was worth the price of admission because he had watched my movies and television shows his whole life. Now, I don't know if they say this to everyone that they meet, or if it's even true, but when people say kind and loving things such as that, it somehow makes everything worthwhile and I feel so blessed.

Me backstage with Bobby Rydell in Las Vegas.

Back to our life in Vegas. I started doing a lot of local television commercials and print work, and eventually I felt that we were truly meant to be there. One day I got a call from my agent regarding an audition for a role in the NBC series *Las Vegas*, starring James Caan and Josh Duhamel, and was thrilled when I got the part. I also got a call from Charles Dennis, who offered me a part in a film called *Hard Four*. It was a small role but he actually wrote it with me in mind, so I was flattered. The movie starred Ross

A poster from the Ted V. Mikels horror movie *Demon Haunt*.
I play a snooping neighbor.

Benjamin, the son of Richard Benjamin and Paula Prentiss. What a sweetie and cutie he was! The movie also starred Ed Asner, Ed Begley Jr., Dabney Coleman, and Paula Prentiss, who's the sweetest lady in the world. I had gone to a screening of *The Greatest Show on Earth* in Los Angeles the year before, and they introduced me to the audience because I was one of the few people in the film who was still alive! It turns out that Charles Dennis had sat behind me in the theater and decided to track me down.

I also did a low-budget film for Ted V. Mikels titled *Demon Haunt* (2008), in which I played an over-the-top nosy neighbor married to a real redneck, played by my friend Rusty Meyers. I was introduced to Ted by Rusty and hired on the spot. In addition, I was asked to appear at the Star Trek Experience at the Las Vegas Hilton almost every weekend, which proved to be a wonderful experience. I signed countless photos for eager fans.

Then the unthinkable happened—my wonderful husband Mike was diagnosed with prostate cancer. I was stunned. How could this be? Everything was going so well. At that instant our world fell apart. I couldn't think. I couldn't function. I wanted to be brave for Mike and not let him see me cry so I went for a walk with our dog, Cookie, everyday to cry and pray, then returned home with a brave face.

Mike never once complained. He was determined to beat the cancer and for awhile it looked as if he would. He always had a smile on his face and every day, when I would tell him that I loved him, he would answer, "I love you more."

When Mike was diagnosed, we didn't have health insurance to pay for his treatments, which were quite expensive. Each shot, which was supposed to keep the cancer from spreading, cost $1,500, and his oncologist wanted to give him one shot each month. We would have paid anything for the treatment, of course, but the point was moot because we had very little money, so panic mode set in. After crying on my good friend Florie's shoulder, as I did so many times, she comforted me and assured me that things would turn out all right.

Florie has always been there for me, as have all of my wonderful friends, and about an hour after we talked, she called back and asked if Mike had served in the military. If so, she reasoned, perhaps the VA could be of assistance. Mike and I were stunned because neither of us had even thought of that. As it turned out, Mike had been in the Navy and served in Vietnam. The VA agreed to pay for everything because it was determined that his cancer had been caused by exposure to Agent Orange, a powerful defoliant. When Mike finally passed away, the VA also made sure that he received a full military funeral. He was cremated and buried in a VA cemetery, and when my time comes, I'll be buried next to him so we can be together forever.

Mike was a proud veteran, and I have a special place in my heart for all of the brave men and women who have served in the military. In fact, two of my nephews—Scott and Kevin—have served in Iraq and Afghanistan. Scott, a Navy medic, has been deployed three times and, as I write this, is facing his fourth. I'm extraordinarily proud of both of them, and I encourage everyone to please say a prayer for them and all service personnel who put their lives on the line to keep this great nation safe.

The doctors gave Mike three months to live, yet miraculously he lived for four more years. We realized that each day was a gift. He cut back on his work because the cancer treatment caused him to tire easily, though he still made sales calls whenever he was able. Because Mike was a Vietnam veteran, his income was supplemented with a disability check from the VA, which helped considerably.

At the end, however, Mike's cancer started to spread, and he grew weaker and weaker. But through it all he was able to maintain the smile that drew me to him when we first met. When Mike finally entered hospice, we were surrounded by my family, his family, and our many wonderful friends. I couldn't have gone through it without their love and support.

One day I asked Mike if he was afraid to die, and he said, "Not as long as you're the last person I see when I take my last breath." I've thought about those words so many times over the years because they make me realize how blessed I was to have a person like Mike in my life. So many people go their entire lives without finding someone to love, and yet I know what it's like to be cherished. When he finally passed, I was holding his hand, so I truly was the last person he saw when he took his last breath, and for that I'm eternally thankful.

Some readers may know my niece, Darlene Tompkins, who starred with Elvis Presley in *Blue Hawaii* (1961). We were always close growing up, but sadly we no longer speak to each other, which is difficult for me to understand because family is so important to me. Those who have lost someone close will understand the despair I felt at Mike's passing. I was lost, empty and unable to feel. I wanted to jump off the nearest cliff. I was truly crazy—screaming, crying constantly, and unable to function. My family and friends stood by me during this period of extraordinary heartbreak—Darlene did not. She couldn't handle my craziness and turned her back on me. I'm deeply saddened by that, but I know deep down that we'll always love each other. We're just not a part of each other's lives anymore.

Through my journey, I've shed many tears, real and "reel," but fortunately I've had much laughter too. Crying can be very healing because it is a natural release and lets you feel. It also releases painkilling brain chemicals called endorphins. The worst thing a person can say to someone is "don't cry," because if you don't cry, you can't feel. Of course, even better than tears is laughter. I've laughed until I cried, and I've cried until I laughed.

Beverly Washburn

Me today, still working, still happy!

And in thinking back, I can't help but believe that it's the laughter that has kept me going. My entire family has been gifted with a wonderful sense of humor. After Mike died, I didn't laugh for a very long time. Now, though, just the thought of his infectious laughter makes me smile.

As I write this, it's been almost four years since Mike passed away. One of my wonderful hospice bereavement counselors said to me, "You'll never get over it, but you will get through it." I've never forgotten that.

I've learned to thank God for what I have, and to trust God for what I need. I will forever have a part of me that is missing, and there will forever be a little hole in my heart, but I've learned to not try to fill that hole. Instead, I embrace it, I acknowledge it, and I keep that little hole in my heart just for Mike, so I'll feel him with me every day.

I'm a firm believer in gratitude, and I have a little ritual that I perform every morning when I wake up. I take three deep breaths, and simply say, "thank you." I then thank God for everything that is important in my life, such as my health, my family, my friends, and my pets. I end by saying, "Thank you for all that I have and for all that I am about to receive." It's simple, but powerful and effective—for me, anyway.

As my story comes to a close, I'd like to think of it more as a beginning. I don't know what God has in store for me around the corner, but I do know that I've had a wonderful life, a wonderful family, wonderful friends, and many beautiful memories. I'm grateful that I'm still working in the business I love, and that life is good once again.

If I were to leave a legacy, I would like it to be that perhaps I've touched someone's life; that I was a good person; that I was compassionate, caring, and kind; that I made people laugh; and that I had a gentle heart. I've had many losses in my life, many ups and downs, but I wouldn't change any of it because it has brought me to where I am today, and I feel truly blessed.

For those of you who have bought this book, thank you for making a dream of mine come true, and for touching MY life.

* * *

A final note...

Many years ago, my mother decided that she wanted to write a book about being the parent of children in show business. It was to be titled "The Trials and Tribulations of a Hollywood Mother." She got as far as getting letters from Jack Benny and Bob Hope, both of whom were very supportive of her effort, but then she developed dementia and was unable to continue. Years later, my sister Audrey and I found the manuscript that our mother had written, and Audrey decided to take up where my mother had left off, only the book would be from the perspective of the sister of a child actress, and contain many photos from my career, which we had kept in a large scrapbook. Sadly, Audrey became ill, and once again the book was put aside. After she died, I was so distraught that I totally forgot that she even had the scrapbook.

Fast forward to 2008, when I ran into Kenny Miller, a fellow actor, at the Memphis Film Festival. Kenny is 12 years older than I am, so we ran in different circles growing up, but I had always been a fan of his and knew exactly who he was as far back as the '60s because he seemed to be in every fan magazine published at the time. Kenny came by my table to say hello and we started talking. One thing led to another, and I mentioned the long-abandoned manuscript that both my mother and sister had tried to write and publish. Kenny immediately suggested that I dust it off and see what I could do with it. My husband, Mike, had wanted me to do this for a very long time, but I wasn't sure where to begin. Kenny introduced me to a wonderful writer by the name of Donald Vaughan, who said he would be more than happy to help me put my thoughts on paper and get the book started. (Don had collaborated with Kenny on his autobiography, *Hollywood Inside & Out: The Kenny Miller Story*, also published by BearManor Media.)

As Don and I were in the preliminary stages of this book, my scrapbook from more than 30 years ago surfaced on eBay! I was baffled because I had no idea who had acquired it since Audrey's passing. I watched the bidding go up and up, and figured that I would never see my scrapbook again. Well, much to my absolute surprise, my former boyfriend, Richard, was also aware of the auction, and bought the scrapbook so I could have it once again. I had no idea that Richard was bidding on it because he used his fictitious eBay name, so when it ended, I thought it was a stranger who had won, a fact that saddened me greatly. A few days after the auction, I went to the mailbox and there it was! I burst into tears, and called Richard right away. He explained to me, "Washburn (his nickname for me forever), you and I did a pinkie swear many years ago that we would always be friends no matter what, and it didn't seem right to me that someone else would have your scrapbook. It belongs to you, so I bought it. That's what friends are for."

I'll never forget Richard's wonderful act of kindness and generosity. Once again, I feel truly blessed. So it is because of Richard that I'm able to share with you all the wonderful photos contained in this book.

Thank you, dear Richard, for your kind and generous heart.